'Changed my life!
I always thought
I couldn't cook,
these books have
changed that.'

Emma Mannus

'Loved every single
recipe. 10/10.'

Charlotte Wood

'Most used cookbooks
in our house.'

Rebecca Jane

'Game changer when
cooking for a family and
want to eat healthily.'

Sarah Lacey

BORED

OF

LUNCH

Healthy Air Fryer

30 MINUTE
MEALS

BORED
OF
LUNCH

Healthy Air Fryer

30 MINUTE
MEALS

NATHAN ANTHONY

EBURY
PRESS

CONTENTS

Introduction

Writing and publishing books still feels quite new to me, so how we're here at our fourth Bored of Lunch book already feels like some sort of dream. Welcome back to my resident lunchers and hello for anyone coming to Bored of Lunch for the first time – I hope you're ready for an air fryer frenzy!

For those who have bought my books before, I want to thank you for your ongoing support. It's down to you that I've been able to write more books, create more recipes and keep doing what I love. THANK YOU.

For any newbies who have just picked up their first BOL book, let me briefly introduce myself. I'm Nathan, I'm from Belfast in Northern Ireland and I'm a busy home cook like you. I'm not a trained chef, I'm just someone who loves food and got stuck in a boring eating rut so decided to start posting recipes online. I couldn't believe how quickly the Bored of Lunch community started to grow, and now I'm here, writing my fourth book in two years and continuing to post recipes to my online followers.

If you already follow me online, you'll know that I love a time-saving gadget and the air fryer is something that has made cooking for me easier, quicker and healthier. Shorter cook times, less costly to run and requiring a fraction of the oil that regular frying methods use – it's no wonder sales of air fryers have continued to climb in recent years.

We all lead busy lives (is it just me that feels like the pace of life is getting faster and faster?!) and often the last thing we have time to do is spend hours making ourselves something to eat. Here's where this book comes in. With every recipe ready in 30 minutes or less, I hope this will give you tons of ideas for how to feed your family quickly, without having to resort to unhealthy ready meals or expensive takeaways.

As with all my previous books, every recipe is calorie counted. Calories are something I find useful to track, and I know a lot of you have found this useful in the past, but these books are for you to tailor to your specific needs. If you fancy a double portion, or you want to add more cheese – you do you. I'm never going to argue with more cheese!

I hope you love this book as much as I do and find yourself flicking through the pages and wondering just what recipe you might start with. I love seeing your recreations on social media, so please come and find me on there and show me what you've been cooking.

Love,
Nathan

NATHAN'S TOP AIR FRYING TIPS

1 Silicone liners placed at the bottom of your air fryer drawer are a perfect way to save on mess and washing-up time. You can buy these online quite cheaply, and can even get ones that will fit your particular air fryer drawer.

2 For anything that has a crispy coating or batter – for example, tempura veg or crispy fish – preheat your air fryer to 200°C for a few minutes. This way, the wet meat, fish or veg hits hot air instantly and you'll get a much crispier result.

3 If you've got fruit that's about to go off, put it in the air fryer on the dehydrate setting and you'll end up with a tasty dried fruit snack that makes a delicious topping for porridge.

4 If you have leftovers, make use of the reheat setting (don't re-air-fry them). I find this especially good for leftover pizza. Three minutes on the reheat setting and it's good as new.

5 Treat your air fryer as you would your oven – anything ovenproof will be air fryer-proof. You can use ceramics, tin foil, baking paper, skewers, all sorts. Just double-check the maximum baking temperature for your ceramics, as air fryers will usually reach up to 220°C.

6 When it comes to cleaning up, I just soak the air fryer drawer/basket in hot soapy water while I eat my food, then scrub and rinse when I'm done. The grill rack inserts can usually go into the dishwasher, too, which is handy if you're really pressed for time.

7 Frozen foods like fish fingers or breaded chicken are so good in an air fryer. You might notice that some brands are adding air fryer times to labels now, but if you're unsure – air fryers usually take around 60% of the time recommended for oven cooking. If a timing says 15 minutes, I'll check it after 10.

8 Some air fryers have a rotisserie-style insert, but I've never found them to do anything better than just setting the chicken in the regular basket.

9 If you're feeding a family, try to get an air fryer that has two drawers so you can do your potatoes or sides in one drawer and your protein in the other.

10 Oil spray is your friend with air fryer cooking. I use low-calorie oil sprays a lot, but for an even crispier result an olive oil spray or a quick drizzle of olive oil work very well as alternatives.

11 Don't overcrowd the basket or pile things on top of one another. Particularly when you're cooking things like meat and fish, you want to see a few empty spots at the bottom of your drawer. The exception to this are things like potatoes and chips – you can slightly overcrowd these in the drawer, but make sure you shake it a few times during cooking, to get an even result.

HOW TO USE THIS BOOK

The recipes in this book have been created to make cooking as fuss-free and easy as possible and, in particular, to reduce the amount of planning. To help with this, I've included some handy symbols so you can see at a glance how long a recipe is going to take to prep and cook. You'll also be able to see if it's veggie or if it's suitable for freezing.

prep time

cook time

vegetarian

freezeable

To be honest, air-fried food is always best eaten freshly cooked, so you'll see far fewer freezer icons in this book than in my slow cooker book. There are still times when it can be useful to freeze, though. Just remember to ensure your food has cooled to room temperature before putting it in the freezer, and then to make sure you reheat everything thoroughly until it's piping hot throughout. Do not refreeze food that has already been defrosted once.

There is a list of my pantry essentials – the ingredients I find it helpful to have in my cupboard – on page 184.

A HEALTHY BALANCE – First things first, this is not a diet book. I don't come from a fitness background and I'm not a nutritionist, but I do track my calories to suit my nutritional needs and goals. There are lots of apps that will recommend your ideal calorie intake based on your height and weight (as a general guide, the NHS recommends 2,000 calories per day for women and 2,500 for men). I find it helpful to know how many calories I'm eating at each meal if I'm trying to tailor my diet to a specific target (and some days, I don't care at all!), so I've made sure to include this for each recipe.

However, I'm a big believer that a healthy diet is a balanced diet. Throughout the book you'll see I use oil, butter, cheese and cream as these are foods I enjoy (regularly!). If you want to, you can tweak the recipes to adjust or remove some of the more calorific ingredients. Similarly, if calorie counting isn't something that's important to you, feel free to make swaps that suit you. For example, if I've suggested serving something with salad but you want to serve it with chips, please do. If I've only used 30g of cheese in a recipe but you are a cheese-lover, please up the amount! I want you to feel able to play around with these recipes so that they suit you.

Finally, if a serving suggestion has been included in the ingredients list (eg, rice, pasta or noodles), then this will be included in the final calorie count. If I've listed something as optional, this isn't included in the total.

FAKEAWAYS

IN

A

FLASH

STICKY SESAME CHICKEN

PER SERVING
509
CALORIES

Sticky honey chicken sprinkled with sesame seeds – this is so good and will have you thinking you're going to town on your calories for the day, when in reality you aren't at all. A healthier, lighter way to enjoy a takeaway favourite, this is great with egg noodles and some steamed pak choi.

SERVES **2**

 10 MIN

 20 MIN

3–4 tbsp cornflour
1 tsp garlic granules
1 tsp onion granules
1 tsp Chinese 5 spice
300g chicken breasts, cut into bite-size chunks
1 egg, beaten
low-calorie oil spray

To garnish
1 tbsp white sesame seeds
2 spring onions, chopped
2 red chillies, finely diced

Sauce
1 tsp sesame oil
2 tbsp soy sauce
3 tbsp honey
2 tbsp sweet chilli sauce
1 tsp rice wine vinegar
½ tsp Chinese 5 spice
2 tbsp sriracha
1 tbsp garlic purée
1 tbsp ginger purée

1   Combine the cornflour and spices in a bowl. Coat the chicken in the beaten egg, then in the spiced cornflour mix. Spray well with the oil spray and air-fry for 14 minutes at 200°C.

2   Mix together the sauce ingredients in a bowl.

3   When the chicken is cooked, pour the sauce over the chicken and air-fry for a further 2–3 minutes until the sauce thickens, or add the sauce to a small pan to warm over a low heat.

4   Once cooked, serve garnished with the sesame seeds, chopped spring onions and red chillies.

FISH & CHIPS

PER SERVING
574
CALORIES

Well, it turns out the key to the best fakeaway fish and chips is a bag of salt and vinegar crisps. Honestly, you won't believe how well this turns out with the crisp crumb on the outside of the fish. In Northern Ireland, we put gravy on our chips, so for me this is unbeatable with mushy peas, tartare sauce and a tub of gravy on the side.

SERVES **2**

 15 MIN

 15 MIN

2 skinless cod fillets
2 tbsp plain flour
1 large egg, beaten
75g salt and vinegar crisps, crushed
frozen chips of choice, or use the recipe on page 142

300g tin of mushy peas, drained
Tartare sauce (optional – see page 48)
salt, to taste

1   Pat the fish dry with kitchen paper and salt it generously. This will help prevent it falling apart during cooking. Place the flour, egg and crushed crisps into three separate bowls.

2   Dunk the fillets first in the flour, then into the beaten egg, then finally into the crisp crumb to coat. Cook the coated fish in the air fryer for 12–14 minutes at 200°C – frozen chips should take the same length of time, so add them all together.

3   Meanwhile, heat the mushy peas in the microwave, then serve with the fish and chips, and tartare sauce, if you wish.

CRISPY FRIED CHICKEN

PER SERVING
411
CALORIES

You know where we're going with this one – yes, that's right, it's the one you're thinking about. I recommend pairing this with air-fried skinny fries and a little pot of baked beans just like the Colonel does. This is a true fakeaway – all the flavour of the original but with fewer calories.

SERVES **6**

 10 MIN

 20 MIN

1.2kg chicken drumsticks and thighs, skin-on
200ml buttermilk or 4 beaten eggs
120g plain flour
120g cornflour
2 tbsp paprika
1 tsp chilli powder
1 tbsp dried oregano
1 tsp dried thyme

1 tsp dried basil
1 tbsp mustard powder
½ tsp ground ginger
1 tbsp garlic granules
1½ tbsp white pepper
1 tbsp black pepper
1 tsp salt
2 tbsp vegetable oil
olive oil spray (not low-calorie)

1   Coat the chicken pieces in the buttermilk or beaten egg.

2   Mix together all the dry ingredients in a bowl, then dredge the chicken first in this mix, then back into the buttermilk or beaten egg, then coat in the dry mix one more time.

3   Add the vegetable oil to your air fryer and preheat for 2 minutes at 200°C.

4   This next step is very important; coat the chicken VERY well with the olive oil spray – the flour needs to look mostly yellow from the spray. Air-fry at 200°C for 20 minutes, turning and re-spraying halfway through cooking.

5   As your air fryer will be at capacity with the chicken, you could just pop some chips in the oven and heat some baked beans in the microwave or on the hob to accompany.

TIP

If you're using buttermilk, you could leave the chicken to marinate in the fridge for 4 hours or overnight for an extra-tender result.

TAKEAWAY-STYLE HONEY & SOY RIBS

PER SERVING
254
CALORIES

This one reminds me of my childhood and me shouting 'HONEY RIBS, PLEASE' while my mum was on the phone ordering the Chinese takeaway. Sticky and sweet, the flavour here is out of this world and so moreish. Serve with steamed rice and greens, or alongside lots of other dishes as part of a sharing feast.

SERVES **6**

 5 MIN

 25 MIN

1kg pork ribs
2 tbsp dark soy sauce, plus 1 tbsp to glaze
1 tbsp Chinese 5 spice
2 tbsp rice wine vinegar
½ tsp garlic salt

½ tsp onion salt
low-calorie oil spray
1 tsp hoisin sauce
3 tbsp honey
2 lemons

1   Place the ribs in a large pan of water and bring to the boil. Simmer for 10 minutes to tenderise, then drain.

2   Coat the ribs in the 2 tablespoons of soy sauce, the Chinese 5 spice, rice wine vinegar and garlic and onion salts along with some oil spray, then air-fry for 10–12 minutes at 200°C.

3   In a bowl, mix the remaining tablespoon of soy sauce with the hoisin, honey and juice of one of the lemons. Glaze the ribs with the sauce and air-fry again for 5 minutes at 200°C.

4   When serving, squeeze the juice of the remaining lemon over the sticky ribs.

TIP

To make your ribs extra tender, you can simmer them in water for 1–1½ hours before coating in the flavourings and crisping in the air fryer.

ORANGE CHICKEN

PER SERVING
344
CALORIES

This chicken is so delicious – somewhere between sweet 'n' sour and a honey chilli dish – and if you already cook from my books, you'll likely have all the ingredients on hand to make this. I use two good-sized chicken breasts, which will be enough for three people or two large portions if you're hungry.

SERVES **2**

  10 MIN

  20 MIN

3 heaped tbsp cornflour
1 tsp garlic granules
1 tsp ground ginger
1 tsp chilli powder
2 chicken breasts, cut into
   bite-size chunks
1 tsp vegetable oil
salt and pepper, to taste
2 spring onions, chopped,
   to garnish

Sauce
100ml smooth orange juice
1 tbsp honey
3 tbsp soy sauce
1 tsp chilli powder
1 tsp ground ginger
2 garlic cloves, crushed

1   Combine the cornflour, garlic granules, ginger and chilli powder with some salt and pepper. Coat the chicken chunks in this mix, remove the air fryer tray and transfer to the basket. Drizzle with the oil. Air-fry for 12–14 minutes at 200°C, shaking the tray halfway through so nothing sticks.

2   Meanwhile, combine all the sauce ingredients in a saucepan and allow to simmer for 5–8 minutes, or until reduced and thickened. Add to the cooked chicken, tossing well to coat, then air-fry at 200°C for a further 3–4 minutes.

3   Serve, garnished with the chopped spring onions.

SERVING NOTE

Serve with rice or air-fried chips. Adding 125g of cooked rice per serving will add 169 calories.

FAKEAWAYS IN A FLASH!

SICHUAN-STYLE PRAWNS & ASPARAGUS

PER SERVING
174
CALORIES

A lot of the recipes I write are inspired by my travels or by places I've eaten at and this recipe is inspired by a local restaurant. My air fryer has two drawers, so I put the prawns in one and the asparagus in the other to make things quicker. If asparagus is out of season, you can sub for Tenderstem broccoli.

SERVES **4**

 10 MIN

 15 MIN

1 tbsp Sichuan peppercorns, roughly crushed (or use black pepper and a pinch of dried chilli flakes)
1 tbsp + 1 tsp sesame oil
2 tbsp dark soy sauce
1 garlic clove, grated
400g raw king prawns
100g asparagus spears, cut in half
1 tsp butter
1 tbsp honey

Sauce
2 tbsp light soy sauce
1 tbsp tomato purée
1 tbsp Shaoxing rice wine
1 tbsp ginger purée
2 garlic cloves, grated

To garnish
1 tbsp sesame seeds
1 red chilli, finely chopped
2 spring onions, finely sliced

1 Combine the peppercorns, the tablespoon of sesame oil, 1 tablespoon of the soy sauce, garlic and some salt and pepper in a bowl. Add the prawns and coat in the marinade. Cook in the air fryer for 6 minutes at 200°C.

2 Combine all the sauce ingredients, then pour over the prawns and air-fry for 2 more minutes, giving the tray a shake.

3 Add the asparagus to a clean air fryer drawer with the butter, the teaspoon of sesame oil and some salt and pepper. Cook for 4 minutes at 200°C. Add the remaining tablespoon of soy and the honey, and fry for 2 minutes more.

4 Serve the prawns alongside the asparagus, garnished with the sesame seeds, chilli and spring onions.

CHAR SIU PORK

PER SERVING
435
CALORIES

Gorgeously charred sticky pork is such a delicious dish and a real fakeaway treat. I do change up what I serve this with as it goes great with noodles or served in bao buns, but sticky rice and some spicy wilted spinach is quite hard to beat as a combo. I hope you love this recipe as much as I do.

SERVES **4**

 5 MIN

 20 MIN

3 tbsp honey
1 tbsp sweet chilli sauce
1 tbsp dark soy sauce
1 tbsp hoisin sauce
1 tsp sesame oil
1 tbsp Shaoxing rice wine
few dashes of red food
    colouring
800g boneless pork shoulder
    or tenderloin (in one piece)
salt and pepper, to taste

To serve
100g sticky rice per person
stir-fried spinach with
    chopped red chilli stirred
    through
sesame seeds, to garnish

1   Combine all the ingredients, except the pork, in a bowl, seasoning with salt and pepper. Reserve 2 tablespoons of the marinade and set aside, then add the pork to the remaining marinade and turn to coat all over. If you've got time, leave it overnight or for up to 4 hours. If not, don't worry, it'll still be delicious.

2   When ready to cook, air-fry for 20 minutes at 200°C.

3   Once cooked, brush the pork with the reserved marinade, then slice and serve with the sticky rice and stir-fried spinach.

TIP
━

If you're using pork shoulder and want it extra tender, cook in the oven at 150°C for 3 hours, then finish in the air fryer for 8–10 minutes at 200°C.

FAKEAWAYS IN A FLASH!

SPICY FETA TURKEY BURGERS

PER SERVING
540
CALORIES

I've no doubt these absolutely gorgeous turkey burgers will become a favourite fakeaway in your house. Turkey mince is lean and has a reputation for being flavourless, but paired with some spices, salty feta, charred corn and a dollop of coleslaw, it can really transform into something completely mouth-watering.

SERVES **4**

 15 MIN

 15 MIN

400g turkey mince
1 tbsp oil
1 tbsp Cajun seasoning
1 tsp onion salt
1 tsp paprika
½ tsp garlic granules
handful of fresh basil leaves, chopped
50g feta cheese
salt and pepper, to taste

To serve
4 brioche buns, toasted
¼ iceberg lettuce, shredded
2 tomatoes, sliced
spicy red cabbage slaw or slaw mixed with sriracha
4 corn on the cob, charred
jalapeños or pickles from a jar (optional)

1   Mix the turkey mince, oil, seasonings, basil, feta and some salt and pepper in a bowl, then divide the mixture into four balls and press down flat into burger shapes. Air-fry the burgers for 7 minutes on each side at 200°C, they should be beautifully coloured.

2   Assemble the burgers in the brioche buns with the lettuce, sliced tomatoes, slaw, corn and jalapeños, if you like, for some extra spice.

MEATBALL MARINARA SUB

PER SERVING
787
CALORIES

My order at a certain high street sandwich shop is pretty much always a foot-long meatball marinara sub, so I had to have a go at making my own using the air fryer. The result is this – meatballs cooked in a beautifully rich marinara sauce piled into a toasted bread roll and topped with oozing cheese.

SERVES **4**

 10 MIN

 20 MIN

Meatballs
300g lean beef mince
300g lean pork mince
80g dried breadcrumbs
1 egg, beaten
1 tsp dried sage
1 tsp dried thyme
salt and pepper, to taste

Marinara sauce
400g good-quality passata

1 tbsp garlic purée
1 tbsp dried oregano
1 tsp onion granules
1 tsp dried chilli flakes

To serve
4 sub rolls or 2 baguettes, halved
1 red onion, sliced
1 red pepper, sliced
8 thin cheese slices

1 Preheat the air fryer to 200°C. Combine all the ingredients for the meatballs in a large mixing bowl, then form into about 12 meatballs using damp hands. Air-fry for 14–16 minutes.

2 While they are cooking, combine all the ingredients for the marinara sauce in a bowl. Add to the air fryer drawer for the final 4 minutes of the meatball cooking time.

3 If your air fryer has a second drawer, toast the bread rolls in it for 3 minutes. If you need to, you can just toast the breads under the grill.

4 Once everything is ready, fill each roll with the garnishes, meatballs and sauce topped with two slices of cheese.

BARBECUE CHICKEN TENDERS

PER SERVING
320
CALORIES

Sticky barbecue chicken in a crispy coating dunked into garlic mayo – this really is the snack sharing food of dreams. Of course, you can make these for lunch, served with potatoes and salad, but put a plate of these down when you've got friends round for a movie night and you'll be the host with the most. Flavour, flavour, flavour!

SERVES **4**

 15 MIN

 15 MIN

100g cornflakes, crushed
2 tbsp paprika
1 tsp garlic granules
2 eggs
4 chicken breasts, each cut
   into 3 strips
5 tbsp shop-bought
   barbecue sauce

2 tbsp honey
salt and pepper, to taste
fresh parsley, chopped,
   to garnish
chopped spring onions,
   to garnish
garlic mayo, to serve

1   Mix the cornflakes with 1 tablespoon of the paprika, the garlic granules and some salt and pepper.

2   In a separate bowl, beat the 2 eggs and stir in the remaining paprika. Coat the chicken in the egg, then in the cornflake mixture. Air-fry the chicken for 11 minutes at 190°C.

3   While the chicken is cooking, mix the barbecue sauce and honey in a small bowl, then brush over the cooked chicken.

4   Air-fry for a further 4 minutes, then reglaze with the remaining barbecue sauce and honey when the chicken is plated. Serve garnished with parsley and spring onions.

5   Get dipping into that garlic mayo.

TANDOORI MASALA-STYLE PORK CHOPS

PER SERVING
377
CALORIES

This is a gorgeously versatile recipe that you can make with all sorts of things. I've gone with pork chops as they're a cheaper option, but lamb chops also work amazingly with these flavours. The chops are charred, spicy and well-seasoned and, even though I know it's not very traditional, I find they go amazingly with the spicy crunch of kimchi. Serve this with other sides of your choice – Bombay potatoes (pictured) go particularly well.

SERVES **4**

 5 MIN

 15 MIN

4 large pork chops
1 tsp vegetable oil
1 onion, sliced
2 tbsp fresh coriander, chopped, to garnish
100g kimchi, to serve

Marinade
1 tsp olive oil
3 tbsp Greek yogurt
1 tbsp ginger purée
1 tsp garlic purée
1 tsp paprika
2 tbsp tandoori masala
1 tsp ground coriander
1 tbsp harissa paste

TIP
—

If you've got time to start this the day before, marinate the pork and chill in the fridge overnight to really amp up the flavour.

1   Preheat the air fryer to 190°C. Mix the marinade ingredients together and then coat the pork chops in the marinade.

2   When you're ready to cook, add the pork chops to the preheated air fryer and air-fry for 15 minutes.

3   Meanwhile, heat the vegetable oil in a frying pan and soften the onions for 10–15 minutes or until starting to caramelise.

4   Plate the onions, place the chops on top, garnish with the coriander and serve with the kimchi alongside, and any sides of your choice.

FILLET OF FISH BRIOCHE

As much as I love a beef or chicken burger, I do love a fish burger from time to time. A bit like a giant fish finger sandwich, this is cod in a crispy coating with a tangy sauce, finished with lettuce and a slice of cheese. It doesn't take a genius to work out which famous fast food chain I've drawn inspiration from on this one – if you're a lover of the original, I think you're going to really like this.

SERVES **4**

 15 MIN

 15 MIN

4 skinless cod fillets
2 heaped tbsp plain flour
2 eggs, beaten
75g panko breadcrumbs
low-calorie oil spray
4 brioche buns, toasted
¼ iceberg lettuce, shredded
4 cheese slices

Sauce
4 tbsp light mayo
4 cornichons, chopped
1 tsp capers, chopped
1 tbsp dill, finely chopped
salt and pepper, to taste

1   Pat the fish dry with kitchen paper. Place the flour, beaten eggs and breadcrumbs in three separate bowls. Coat the fish first in the flour, then in the egg, then in the breadcrumbs. Spray the coated fillets really well with the oil spray and air-fry for 12–14 minutes at 200°C.

2   Combine all the sauce ingredients in a bowl, seasoning with salt and pepper, to taste.

3   Layer up the buns with the sauce, lettuce, crispy fish, then a cheese slice on top – perfection.

CHICKEN TIKKA FRIED ROTI ROLL

PER SERVING
438
CALORIES

This is something truly special. Inspired, of course, by a very popular Indian restaurant chain that is notorious for their breakfast naans, but here we have something more lunch orientated. Air-fried chicken tikka with a herby and zesty yogurt, stuffed inside a roti that's been briefly fried so it's slightly crispy on the outside. Simply heaven.

SERVES **4**

 10 MIN

 20 MIN

300g fat-free Greek yogurt
1 tsp ground cumin
1 tsp ground turmeric
1 tsp ground coriander
1 tsp garam masala
1 tbsp garlic purée
1 tbsp ginger purée
1 tsp curry powder
1 tbsp mango chutney
400g boneless and skinless chicken thighs
4 shop-bought large rotis

¼ iceberg lettuce, shredded
4 tsp chilli jam
low-calorie oil spray
salt and pepper, to taste

Herb mayo
6 tbsp light mayo
2 tbsp fresh coriander, finely chopped
1 tbsp fresh mint, finely chopped
zest and juice of 1 lime

TIP
—

This will be even better if you have time to leave the chicken to marinate in the yogurt and spices for 4 hours or overnight.

1   Mix the yogurt with the dry seasonings and spices, along with the mango chutney and some salt and pepper. Coat the chicken in the yogurt mix, then cook in the air fryer for 12–14 minutes at 200°C.

2   While the chicken cooks, make the gorgeous herb mayo by combining all the ingredients in a bowl.

3   Once the chicken is cooked, slice into bite–size pieces and fill the rotis with the lettuce, chilli jam, chicken and mayo. Roll tightly, spray with oil and air-fry again for 4 minutes at 200°C. Serve immediately with extra herb mayo and chilli jam on the side, if you like.

CHICKEN FRIED RICE

PER SERVING
455
CALORIES

Who doesn't love fried rice? Here's a quick and cost-effective way to make it. I'm not a massive fan of egg in my fried rice so I've left it as optional in this recipe, but feel free to add it if that's your thing. I use packets of microwaveable rice for ease, but you can prepare it however you like best or use leftover rice if you have any.

SERVES **4**

 10 MIN

 15 MIN

3 chicken breasts, cubed
low-calorie oil spray
1 heaped tsp curry powder
2 x 250g packets of
   microwaveable rice
1 tbsp hoisin sauce
1 tbsp oyster sauce
1 tbsp soy sauce
1 tsp sesame oil
1 tbsp garlic purée

1 tsp ground ginger
½ tsp Chinese 5 spice
1 carrot, grated
1 onion, finely chopped
50g frozen peas
1 egg, beaten (optional)
salt, to taste
50g jar of curry sauce
   and chopped spring
   onions, to serve

1   Preheat the air fryer to 200°C for 2 minutes. Meanwhile, spray the chicken with oil, then dust with the curry powder and season with salt. Add the chicken to the preheated air fryer and air-fry for 7–8 minutes.

2   Cook the rice according to the packet instructions, then toss into the chicken with the hoisin, oyster and soy sauces, the sesame oil, garlic purée, ground ginger and Chinese 5 spice. Toss together along with the veg, then air-fry at 200°C for another 5 minutes.

SERVING NOTE

This will make four large portions or it will serve five as a side dish.

3   If you want to add an egg, do it as soon as the dish is cooked and piping hot. Stir everything through in the air fryer so the egg cooks in the heat of the other ingredients.

4   Serve with some curry sauce and chopped spring onions.

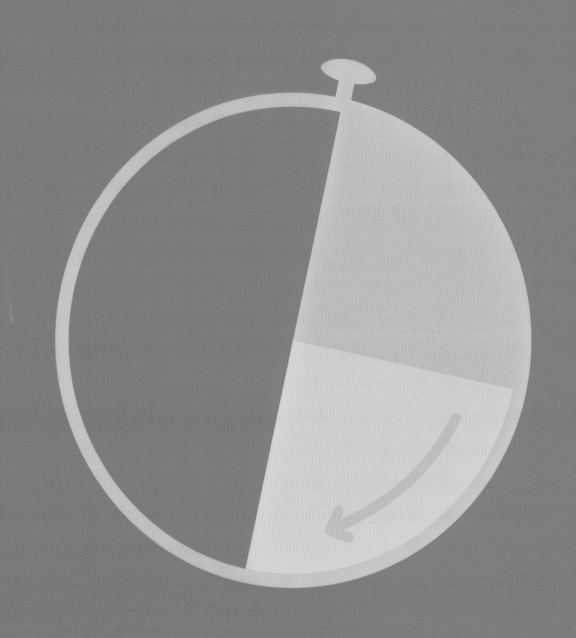

MIDWEEK

MEALS

IN

MINUTES

CHICKEN SCHNITZEL

PER SERVING
410
CALORIES

Pancake-thin chicken coated in crispy breadcrumbs served with buttery mash and a salad makes the perfect midweek meal. Flattening the chicken like this makes it cook really quickly without drying out and it's just divine. Play around with whatever sides you like – have it with salad and coleslaw if you're having a low carb day, or serve with cubed air-fried potatoes. However you serve it, you won't be disappointed.

SERVES **4**

 10 MIN

 15 MIN

4 chicken breasts
90g plain flour
1 tsp paprika
100g panko breadcrumbs
50g Parmesan, grated

1 large egg
low-calorie oil spray
fresh parsley, chopped,
   to garnish
lime wedges and aioli,
   to serve

1   Place the chicken breasts in between two sheets of baking paper, then bang the life out of them with a rolling pin so they are incredibly flat – the thinner the better.

2   Mix the flour and paprika together in one bowl, then in a separate bowl combine the breadcrumbs and Parmesan. Beat the egg in a third bowl. Coat the chicken in the flour first, then in the beaten egg, shaking off any excess, then roll in the breadcrumb mix to coat. Spray well with oil spray and air-fry for 15 minutes at 200°C so they are really crispy.

3   Garnish with parsley, then serve with lime wedges, aioli and your side of choice.

STICKY HOISIN PORK MEATBALLS

Meatballs in a tomato sauce with pasta is obviously a midweek classic, but have you ever had meatballs with a hoisin sauce? Great with rice or noodles, these sticky pork meatballs are perfect for a quick dinner when you have no energy to cook. You can make these even easier by buying those packets of microwaveable rice.

SERVES **4**

 15 MIN

 15 MIN

Meatballs
500g lean pork mince
1 tbsp panko breadcrumbs
1 egg
1 tsp ginger purée
1 tsp garlic purée
low-calorie oil spray

Sauce
3 tbsp hoisin sauce
2 tbsp honey
1 tbsp smooth orange juice
1 tbsp rice wine vinegar

1 tbsp sriracha
1 tsp ground ginger
1 tbsp dark soy sauce

To serve
cooked egg noodles or boiled
    or air-fried rice
julienned cucumber and/or
    carrot
fresh green chilli, finely
    chopped
1 tsp black and white sesame
    seeds

1 In a bowl, mix together all the meatball ingredients, except the oil spray, and then roll into meatballs.

2 Remove the tray from the air fryer basket, add the meatballs and spray with oil. Air-fry for 8–10 minutes at 200°C.

3 Mix together the sauce ingredients and then drizzle over the meatballs, stirring to coat. Cook for a further 3–4 minutes, or until the sauce is reduced and sticky.

4 Serve with the noodles or rice and vegetables, with the chilli and sesame seeds sprinkled over.

FISH CAKES
with Tartare Sauce

PER SERVING
384
CALORIES

Fish cakes really remind me of my childhood, but I don't always remember them being as good as this! I like to use fish poached in milk to make my fish cakes, the end result is flaky cod cooked to perfection. This is a great salad but you can also put the fish cakes and sauce in a brioche bun with some lettuce for a take on a fish finger sandwich.

SERVES **4**

 10 MIN

 20 MIN

2 potatoes, peeled
300g skinless cod fillets
250ml milk
3 garlic cloves, peeled
2 bay leaves
1 tsp parsley, finely chopped
1 tsp dill, finely chopped
75g plain flour
1 egg, beaten
80g panko breadcrumbs
    (more if fish cakes are
    larger)

low-calorie oil spray
salt and pepper, to taste
salad of choice, to serve
    (optional)

Tartare sauce
1 tsp Dijon mustard
1 tbsp capers, chopped
2 tbsp light mayo
4 tbsp Greek yogurt
1 tbsp dill, finely chopped
juice of 1 lemon

1   Cook the potatoes in a pan of boiling water for 10 minutes, drain, then mash and set aside.

2   At the same time, poach the fish in the milk with the garlic, bay leaves and some salt and pepper, in a saucepan over a low-medium heat for 7–10 minutes.

3   Remove the fish from the poaching liquid, then combine the mash and the cooked fish in a bowl, season, add in the parsley and dill, and shape into four cakes. Set the flour, egg and breadcrumbs into three separate bowls. Dip the fish cakes first into the flour, then into the egg, shaking off any

excess, then into the panko breadcrumbs to coat evenly. Spray with the oil spray and air-fry for 10 minutes at 200°C.

4   Combine all the tartare sauce ingredients in a bowl and serve with the fish cakes and a salad. Gorgeous.

TIP

The uncooked fish cakes will freeze really well if you want to prep a batch of these ahead of time.

CHICKEN FAJITA WRAPS

EACH
626
CALORIES

These air-fried chicken fajita wraps look quite basic but are so tasty. I love these for a work-from-home lunch or for whenever that fajita mood grabs me. This recipe will make two full wraps, so if you're cooking for more or fewer people just adjust the quantities accordingly. You don't have to serve the chicken and peppers in wraps either, you could serve them with tacos, rice or whatever you fancy.

MAKES **2**

 5 MIN

 20 MIN

2 chicken breasts, sliced
1 red pepper, sliced
1 yellow pepper, sliced
1 red chilli, sliced
1 tbsp olive oil
1 tsp garlic granules
1 tsp ground cumin
1 tbsp paprika

1 tsp Cajun seasoning
1 tsp ground coriander
salt, to taste
2 large tortilla wraps
100g guacamole (shop-bought or homemade), to serve
100g soured cream, to serve

1 Coat the chicken, peppers and chilli in the oil, flavourings and salt. Air-fry at 200°C for 15 minutes, shaking twice.

2 Remove the chicken, peppers and chilli from the air fryer, add to the wraps and roll up. Return to the same air fryer drawer you cooked the chicken in and air-fry again for 5 minutes at 200°C.

3 Serve with bowls of guacamole and soured cream alongside.

CAPRESE CHICKEN

I have to apologise to my Italian followers for this one. I've taken one of their most famous salads and basically just shoved it inside a chicken breast. It's so delicious though, I'm afraid it's here to stay and I predict it's one you'll be making time and time again. If you want to make this for more people and your air fryer isn't big enough, you can also bake this in the oven for 20–25 minutes at 180°C.

SERVES **2**

 10 MIN

 20 MIN

15 cherry tomatoes, halved
2 tbsp balsamic vinegar
1 tbsp olive oil
2 chicken breasts
1 tsp paprika or
   Cajun seasoning
2 large tomatoes, sliced and
   cut into thin slices

125g mozzarella, drained
   and cut into slices
handful of fresh basil leaves
1 tbsp balsamic glaze
salt and pepper, to taste
salad and fresh bread, to
   serve (optional)

1   Line the base of an ovenproof dish with the cherry tomatoes, then drizzle over the balsamic vinegar and olive oil and sprinkle over some salt and pepper. Toss to mix.

2   Slice the chicken breasts as if you were making hasselback potatoes, then coat them with the paprika or Cajun seasoning. Fill the cuts you have made in the chicken with the tomato and mozzarella slices and a few basil leaves. Place the chicken on top of the tomato mixture and air-fry for 20 minutes at 180°C.

3   Drizzle with the balsamic glaze and serve with salad and fresh bread, if you like.

CHICKEN SHAWARMA FLATBREADS

PER SERVING
425
CALORIES

These are absolutely stunning. This recipe serves four, but on a hungry day I'll make this for two of us and we'll have two each! Packed with powerful flavours and the char from the chicken alongside a gorgeous salad and minty yogurt dressing, everything about this just tastes so clean and fresh. I *highly* recommend.

SERVES **4**

10 MIN

15 MIN

600g boneless and skinless
   chicken thighs
1 tsp paprika
1 tsp ground turmeric
1 tbsp ground cumin
½ tsp mild chilli powder
1 garlic clove, grated
1 tsp olive oil
juice of 1 lemon
salt and pepper, to taste
4 warmed flatbreads,
   to serve

Salad
½ iceberg lettuce, chopped
1 cucumber, sliced
1 celery stick, chopped
1 red onion, sliced
handful of sundried
   tomatoes, chopped

Yogurt dressing
150g fat-free Greek yogurt
zest and juice of 1 lime
handful of fresh mint or
   coriander, chopped
1 garlic clove, minced

1 Coat the chicken in the spices, garlic, olive oil, lemon juice and seasoning and air-fry for 15 minutes at 200°C.

2 While the chicken is cooking, combine all the salad ingredients in a big serving bowl, and mix together all the ingredients for the yogurt dressing in a small bowl.

3 Roughly chop the cooked chicken and serve alongside the bowls of salad and dressing with the warmed flatbreads for everyone to assemble themselves.

PORK SOUVLAKI FLATBREADS
with a Greek Salad

PER SERVING
615
CALORIES

If you've read any of my previous books, you'll know how much I love the food in Greece. Souvlaki literally means 'small skewer', but on a menu it refers to a dish of skewered meat, and I've eaten it in every form – pork, veal, lamb, beef and chicken. Here is a pork version, but you can use any of the alternative meats mentioned. You can use metal or wooden skewers for this, but if you go with wooden ones I recommend soaking them for 30 minutes before using, so they don't burn.

SERVES **4**

 15 MIN

 15 MIN

TIP
—

If you have time, leave the pork to sit in the marinade for 30 minutes before adding to the air fryer, for extra flavour.

700g pork tenderloin
4 flatbreads
salt and pepper, to taste

Marinade
1 tbsp olive oil
1 tbsp dried oregano
1 tbsp dried basil
juice and zest of 1 lemon
juice of 1 lime
1 tbsp red wine vinegar
1 tbsp honey
1 tbsp paprika

Tzatziki
¼ cucumber, grated and squeezed to remove excess liquid
1 tbsp fresh mint, finely chopped
1 garlic clove, grated
6 tbsp fat-free Greek yogurt

1   Cut the pork into bite-size pieces. Combine the marinade ingredients in a bowl, then add the pork and coat.

2   Preheat the air fryer to 190°C for 5 minutes. Thread the pork onto skewers and then air-fry for 15 minutes. For the last 2 minutes of the cooking time, add in your flatbreads so they are nice and toasty.

3 Combine the tzatziki ingredients in a small bowl.

4 Serve the pork skewers with the tzatziki and flatbreads.

SERVING NOTE

This goes amazingly with a simple Greek salad on the side.

BUFFALO CHICKEN BURGERS
with a Garlic & Blue Cheese Ranch

PER SERVING
885
CALORIES

Buffalo chicken and blue cheese dressing – is there any better combination? I didn't think there was until I combined the dressing with some garlic ranch and let me tell you, it's off the scale good. These chicken burgers are amazing but that dressing really does take them to another level. So easy to make, serve them with some air-fried chips when you're in the mood for a takeaway.

SERVES **2**

 15 MIN

 15 MIN

75g cornflakes, crushed

1 tsp paprika

1 tsp onion granules

1 tsp garlic granules

2 chicken breasts, cut in half or flattened

75g fat-free Greek yogurt

low-calorie oil spray

120ml hot sauce mixed with 1 tbsp honey

2 brioche baps, cut in half

¼ iceberg lettuce, shredded

1 red onion, thinly sliced

Garlic and blue cheese ranch dressing

150g fat-free Greek yogurt

5 garlic cloves, grated or minced

4 tbsp light mayo

1 tbsp honey

fresh chives, chopped

30g blue cheese, finely crumbled

salt and pepper, to taste

1   Mix together the cornflakes, paprika and onion and garlic granules. Dip the halved or flattened chicken breasts into the Greek yogurt, then roll in the cornflake mixture to coat. Spray with the oil spray and air-fry for 12 minutes at 180°C. Coat the chicken in the hot sauce and honey mix. Air-fry for a further 3–4 minutes.

2   Combine all the garlic and blue cheese ranch dressing
ingredients, blitzing in a blender if needed.

3   Assemble the burgers by loading up the brioche baps with
the lettuce, onion slices, crispy chicken and a good dollop of
the garlic and blue cheese ranch dressing.

TIP

If garlic and blue cheese dressing isn't your thing,
spicy mayo would make a delicious replacement.

MEATBALL & MOZZARELLA ORZO BAKE

PER SERVING
438
CALORIES

This is a brilliant one-pot dish that involves making orzo in your air fryer. Yes, I know that sounds crazy but please trust the process. With no need to brown your meatballs in a pan first and no extra pots for your pasta, you'll have hardly any washing-up for this and it's brilliantly quick for a pasta bake, too. Cheesy meatball goodness in just 30 minutes.

SERVES **4**

 10 MIN

 20 MIN

400g lean beef mince
2 tbsp panko breadcrumbs
1 onion, finely chopped
handful of fresh basil leaves, chopped
1 egg
2 x 400g tins of chopped tomatoes or 700g passata
1 tbsp tomato purée

1 tbsp balsamic vinegar
1 tbsp honey
4 garlic cloves, crushed
handful of fresh basil leaves, plus extra to garnish
350ml hot chicken stock
175g orzo
60g mozzarella, torn
salt and pepper, to taste

TIP

If you want really oozy mozzarella on top, you could scatter it over while still in the air fryer and air-fry for a further 4 minutes.

1   Combine the mince, breadcrumbs, onion, chopped basil and egg together in a large bowl, then mould into meatballs. Air-fry the meatballs for 7 minutes at 200°C, then add in the tomatoes/passata, tomato purée, balsamic vinegar, honey, garlic, basil, salt and pepper, and cook for a further 3 minutes. If you have a large air fryer, you can do this in an ovenproof dish; if not, use the air fryer basket without the tray in place.

2   Pour in the hot chicken stock, then move the meatballs to one side, add in the orzo and readjust so the meatballs are evenly spread. Air-fry for a further 10 minutes.

3   Top with mozzarella, allowing the residual heat to melt it slightly. Garnish with fresh basil and serve with a side salad.

CHICKEN FLORENTINE
in a Creamy Sauce

Chicken Florentine is a French dish and typically includes cooked spinach and a sauce made with double cream and butter. Here I've made a version with all the same flavours but without the cream and butter, making it less rich and lower in calories. I love this with mash and veg, but it also works really well with a wide, flat pasta such as pappardelle or tagliatelle – the choice is yours.

SERVES **4**

  10 MIN

 20 MIN

4 chicken breasts
1 egg, beaten
150g panko or dried
   breadcrumbs
1 tsp each dried basil and
   oregano
1 tsp olive oil
1 onion, sliced
100g mushrooms, sliced

4 garlic cloves, chopped
200ml milk
100ml chicken stock
juice of ½ lemon
1 tsp dried Italian herbs
2 tbsp soft cream cheese
1 tbsp cornflour
100g baby spinach
salt and pepper, to taste

1   Place the chicken breasts in between two sheets of baking paper, then bang the life out of them with a rolling pin so they are incredibly flat – the thinner the better.

2   Place the beaten egg in one bowl, then combine the breadcrumbs, basil, oregano and some salt and pepper in another. Coat the chicken breasts first in the egg and then in the breadcrumbs. Air-fry for 15 minutes at 200°C.

3   While the chicken is air-frying, heat the olive oil in a wide frying pan and soften the onion for 4–5 minutes. Add the mushrooms and garlic, and cook for another minute. Over a low heat, stir in the milk, chicken stock, lemon juice, some seasoning, the dried herbs and cream cheese, bring to a

simmer and cook for 3–4 minutes. Stir in the cornflour mixed with a tablespoon of water to help thicken the sauce, and then pop in the spinach and cook until wilted.

4   When the chicken is ready, serve with mash and veg or with pasta – it works so well with either.

TIP

If you want to make this even faster, you can use breaded chicken breasts and skip the prep in the first two steps, then air-fry as directed

FIERY MOROCCAN CHICKEN & COUSCOUS

PER SERVING
425
CALORIES

This light but filling meal is one of my go-tos when I'm short on time. Spiced chicken in a fiery sauce with a sweet couscous salad – you can't really go wrong. My tip here is to preheat the air fryer so you get a slight char on the chicken. The couscous salad with sundried tomato and pomegranate is a really nice way to balance the heat in the rest of the dish.

SERVES **4**

 10 MIN

 20 MIN

4 chicken breasts, butterflied
1 tbsp olive oil
1 tbsp garlic purée
1 tsp ground cumin
1 tsp paprika
1 tsp dried oregano
1 tsp ground turmeric
1 tsp onion granules
juice of 1 lemon
salt and pepper, to taste

Couscous

150g couscous
1 tbsp ground turmeric
150ml hot chicken stock
50g sundried tomatoes, chopped

1 tbsp dried fruit (sultanas or raisins are good)
½ cucumber, chopped
2 tbsp pomegranate seeds
1 tbsp balsamic vinegar
handful of fresh basil, chopped

Sauce

3 tbsp tomato purée
2 tbsp soft cream cheese
100ml chicken stock
1 tsp mild chilli powder
½ tsp cayenne pepper
2 tbsp hot sauce

1   Preheat the air fryer to 200°C. Combine the chicken with the oil, garlic purée, spices, onion granules, lemon juice and seasoning. Add to the air fryer and air-fry for 15–17 minutes.

2   Add the couscous, turmeric and hot stock to a heatproof bowl, stir, then cover with cling film and set aside while the chicken is cooking.

3   When the chicken is nearly done, mix together the sauce ingredients in a bowl and season with a little salt, then heat in the microwave for 2–3 minutes or in a pan over a low heat.

4   Add the remaining ingredients to the couscous, fluff up the grains with a fork, slice the chicken and serve both with a salad of your choice and the sauce spooned over.

TIP
—

If you don't like things too spicy, omit the cayenne pepper and reduce the hot sauce.

QUICK COMFORT

STEAK TACOS
with an Avocado Crema

I have said this before, but I could eat tacos every day of the week – whether it's a breakfast taco, fish taco, steak taco, it doesn't really matter. Making them in the air fryer means you can get these done super quickly and, even better, your house won't be left with that cooking smell you get from pan-frying.

MAKES **10**

10 MIN

15 MIN

400g steak (sirloin, rump, any cut will do)
1 tsp vegetable oil or low-calorie oil spray
2 tbsp steak seasoning
1 tsp Cajun seasoning
10 soft-shell tacos
salt and pepper, to taste

Avocado crema
2 ripe avocados
1 green chilli, roughly chopped
1 tbsp fresh coriander, roughly chopped
juice of 1 lime
juice of 1 lemon
4 tbsp Greek yogurt
2 tbsp light mayo
1 garlic clove, peeled

To garnish
150g pickled red onions
50g sundried tomatoes, roughly chopped
coriander, roughly chopped

1   Preheat the air fryer to 200°C. Meanwhile, brush/spray the steaks well with the oil or oil spray, season with salt and pepper, and then rub the dry seasonings evenly all over. Air-fry for 8 minutes, until pink in the middle.

2   While the steaks are sizzling in your air fryer, blitz together all the ingredients for the avocado crema in a food processor to a smooth paste. Transfer to a serving bowl.

3   Allow the steaks to rest for 5 minutes, then slice and serve with the avocado crema, tacos and garnishes. I like to char the tacos directly over the flame on my gas hob for extra flavour before serving.

HAM & CHEESE CROISSANT BOMBS

EACH
315
CALORIES

One of my first ever viral recipes was the Chocolate Egg Croissant Ball (you can find the recipe in my first air fryer book), but here I've made a savoury version with ham and cheese. These are so simple and quick to make – the perfect lazy, throw-together lunch. These work well with so many different flavours. Replace the ham and Dijon with basil pesto or some tomato sauce and dried oregano for delicious vegetarian options.

MAKES **6**

10
MIN

10
MIN

1 packet of croissant pastry (I use Jus-Rol) or 320g ready-rolled puff pastry sheet
1 tbsp Dijon mustard
3 slices of ham, halved

6 small balls of cheese such as mozzarella pearls, or 3 halved Babybels
1 egg, beaten

1   Cut the croissant dough or puff pastry into six triangles and spread a little Dijon mustard onto each triangle.

2   Wrap a half-slice of ham around each cheese ball to keep it safe and prevent it oozing out during cooking. Then wrap a pastry triangle around a cheese ball to form a croissant shape or a ball. Repeat with the other ham-wrapped cheese balls. Glaze each with beaten egg all over, then air-fry for 7–8 minutes at 180°C.

TIP
—

Croissant pastry can be hard to find. Not to worry, you can buy a sheet of ready-rolled puff pastry and cut it into six triangles before wrapping individually.

STUFFED CHICKEN & BACON

This is a proper trip down memory lane, and such a childhood bit of grub for me. My mum made these, and while stuffed chicken breast is no doubt a classic, the stuffing goes well inside any meat. There are a couple of options here, one with a barbecue sauce glaze and the other served with some peppercorn sauce. Both are fantastic!

SERVES **4**

 10 MIN

 20 MIN

4 medium chicken breasts
16 rashers of smoked streaky bacon (don't use thick bacon)
300g stuffing mix

350g Tenderstem broccoli
150g shop-bought peppercorn sauce or
4 tbsp barbecue sauce

1   Slice the chicken breasts along the long side to create a pocket, then fill with the stuffing and tightly wrap each in four of the bacon rashers. Air-fry for 15–17 minutes at 190°C, covering with foil if the bacon starts to get too dark.

2   While the chicken is cooking, steam the broccoli until tender.

3   Once cooked, remove from the air fryer and serve with the broccoli and warmed peppercorn sauce, if using.

4   Alternatively, if serving with barbecue sauce, brush each cooked chicken breast with 1 tablespoon of barbecue sauce and air-fry for a further 2–3 minutes before serving.

SERVING NOTE

This is also great with some mash or air-fried chips, if you're feeling hungry.

STICKY GINGER & SWEET CHILLI CHICKEN STIR FRY

This is a cracking dish that gives you crispy sticky ginger chicken with a chilli sauce and all the things you would expect in a stir fry, but it's made that little bit more simple. You could pan-fry the chicken instead of air-frying it but the air-frying does mean it becomes extra crispy. I love this with noodles, but you could swap for rice or just some steamed greens if you prefer.

SERVES **4**

10 MIN

20 MIN

2 heaped tbsp cornflour
1 tsp ground ginger
1 tsp garlic granules
300g chicken breasts, cubed
low-calorie oil spray
1 red pepper, sliced
1 green pepper, sliced
1 onion, sliced
225g tin of bamboo shoots, drained
150g beansprouts

300g cooked noodles
salt and pepper, to taste

Sauce
2 tbsp honey
3 tbsp sweet chilli sauce
1 tsp sesame oil
2 tbsp soy sauce
2 tbsp ginger purée
1 tbsp garlic purée

1   Combine the cornflour, ground ginger, garlic granules and some salt and pepper in a bowl, then add the chicken and turn to coat. Spray with oil and air-fry for 12 minutes at 200°C.

2   Add the peppers, onion, bamboo shoots and beansprouts to the chicken and air-fry for 5 minutes at 200°C.

3   Meanwhile, combine all the sauce ingredients in a bowl.

4   Add the sauce to the chicken and vegetables, stir, then air-fry for a further 3 minutes, or until thickened, before stirring in the noodles. Enjoy.

SAUSAGE, BEAN & CHEESE MELTS

EACH
646
CALORIES

There are some recipes in the book that veer towards fancy (check out my Garlic Butter Lobster Tails on page 174). Sometimes I'm in the mood for properly cooking and making myself something a little extra special, but other days I'm all about quick, comforting and cheap. This recipe for a cheesy, beany, sausage melt is for those days.

MAKES **3**

 15 MIN

 15 MIN

320g ready-rolled puff pastry sheet
2–3 cooked regular or cocktail sausages (I use low fat) or 150g cooked ham, cut into chunks

150g tin of baked beans
60g Cheddar cheese, grated
1 egg, beaten

TIP
—
To make this cheaper and even quicker, you can buy those tins of beans that have sausages already in them and simply mix with the cheese in step 2.

1   Unroll the puff pastry and divide into six even rectangles.

2   In a bowl, mix the sausage or ham chunks with the baked beans and cheese, then divide the filling between three of the puff pastry rectangles, leaving a 1cm border around the edge.

3   Brush the outer rim of each pastry with the beaten egg and cover with one of the remaining three pastry rectangles, pressing down with a fork to seal. Brush the tops with the beaten egg. Slash the top of each a couple of times with a knife. If you have time to chill the uncooked pastries in the fridge for 10 minutes, it will improve the end result.

4   Transfer the pastries onto strips of baking paper (this will help with removing them when they're hot and fragile) and air-fry at 200°C for 10–12 minutes and get ready to enter cheesy, beany, sausage melt heaven.

SPICED LAMB MINCE
with Flatbreads

PER SERVING
430
CALORIES

This is a dish I could very happily eat once a week and never ever get bored with. It is a bit of a treat because it uses lamb mince, but it's a treat that you need. I always serve this with pre-made Lebanese-style flat breads called Paninette, but whatever flatbreads you can get hold of will work well. You could even make your own using a simple yogurt and flour recipe.

SERVES **4**

 10 MIN

 15 MIN

Lamb
500g lean lamb mince
1 tsp ground cumin
1 tsp ground allspice
1 tsp curry powder
1 tsp ground coriander
1 tbsp tomato purée
1 shallot, finely chopped
½ tsp grated nutmeg
½ tsp paprika
½ tsp dried mint
½ tsp ground cinnamon
1 tbsp oil

Yogurt
5 tbsp Greek yogurt
1 green chilli, finely chopped
handful of fresh coriander, finely chopped
salt and pepper, to taste

To serve
4 Lebanese breads (Paninette) or any flatbreads
fresh coriander
toasted pine nuts

1   Coat the lamb in all those gorgeous flavourings, drizzle over the oil and then stir to mix and break up the mince. Air-fry for 12–14 minutes at 200°C, stirring halfway through.

2   While the meat is cooking, place the breads on a sheet of foil, add a few sprinkles of water, fold the foil to make a parcel, then add to the air fryer at 200°C for 2 minutes.

3   Combine all the yogurt ingredients in a bowl and season.

4   Serve the lamb on top of the breads, then drizzle with yogurt, scatter with the coriander and pine nuts, and enjoy.

TUNA BAGEL MELT

A bit like the pizza bagels from my first air fryer book, these are so simple it doesn't feel quite right calling them a recipe. They make a great light lunch, or sometimes a really filling snack on one of those hungry working-from-home days. If you're just making these for yourself, you can of course simply halve the quantities.

SERVES **2**

  5 MIN

  15 MIN

80g chorizo, cut into cubes or grated (optional)
145g tin of tuna in spring water, drained
3 tbsp light mayo

70g light mozzarella or Cheddar cheese, grated
2 tbsp hot sauce
2 bagels
1 tsp black sesame seeds (optional)

1   Fry the chorizo, if using, in a small frying pan until cooked through and then set aside to cool.

2   In a bowl, combine the tuna, mayo, cheese, hot sauce and cooked chorizo, if using.

3   Slice the bagels in half and top with the mix, sprinkle over the sesame seeds, if using, then air-fry at 190°C for 8–10 minutes. Serve hot.

CHICKEN BREASTS STUFFED with Garlic & Herb Cream Cheese

PER SERVING
490
CALORIES

I worry that there are people out there walking the streets that have never had Boursin. If you're one of those people, prepare to meet your next obsession. I use this cheese in soups and pasta, but stuffed inside a chicken breast with a crispy coating, oozing and melting from the inside, is one of my all-time favourites.

SERVES **4**

 15 MIN

 15 MIN

4 chicken breasts

150g garlic and herb cream cheese (I use Boursin)

100g panko breadcrumbs or crushed cornflakes

1 tbsp Cajun seasoning

4 tbsp plain flour

1 egg, beaten

low-calorie oil spray

salt and pepper, to taste

1   Make an incision in the chicken breasts, but don't slice all the way through, and then fill each one with a quarter of the cream cheese.

2   In a shallow bowl, combine the breadcrumbs or cornflakes with the Cajun seasoning and a pinch of salt and pepper. Put the flour and egg in two separate shallow bowls.

3   Coat the chicken breasts first in the flour, then dip them into the egg, then into the breadcrumbs/cornflakes mix to coat. Spray with the oil and air-fry for 15 minutes at 200°C.

SERVING NOTE

This is perfect with some air-fried cubed potatoes and a salad.

JUICY PORK ROAST & VEG DINNER

PER SERVING
460
CALORIES

A full roast dinner made in one drawer in your air fryer – talk about comfort food that doesn't take you hours in the kitchen. The pork cooks resting on top of your veg and potatoes, making it so easy – and it saves on washing-up. By the end, the outside of the meat is slightly sticky with a beautiful rich flavour from the herbs and the sprouts will have hoovered up some of the juices. Stunning.

SERVES **2**

 10 MIN

 20 MIN

½ tsp dried rosemary
½ tsp dried oregano
½ tsp paprika
½ tsp mustard powder
½ tsp garlic powder
350g pork tenderloin

Veg
2 carrots, cut into batons
pinch of grated nutmeg
1 tsp butter

100g Brussels sprouts
150g potatoes, skin on, cut
    into small cubes

Sticky glaze
2 tbsp honey
1 garlic clove, minced
1 tbsp Dijon mustard
1 tbsp dark soy sauce

1   Combine all the dry flavourings in a bowl, then add the pork and coat all over with the dry rub.

2   Dust the carrots with the nutmeg, place in the bottom of the air fryer, top with the butter, then add the sprouts and potatoes, but keep them all separate – put the potatoes to one side of the basket. Add a layer of foil over the veg and put the pork on top. Air-fry for 10 minutes at 200°C.

3   Remove the foil from the veg, then set the pork on top of the sprouts so the potatoes can get a blast of heat.

4   Combine all the ingredients for the sticky glaze in a bowl and pour on top of the pork, then air-fry for another 10 minutes. Perfection!

BANGERS, ONIONS & GRAVY

PER SERVING
370
CALORIES

Wholesome comfort food doesn't get any better than this. When I think back to my childhood, this was a recipe my granda would have made me when I was at my grandparents' house and I've loved it ever since. I remove the griddle from the air fryer basket for this one so it becomes a true air fryer all-in-one.

SERVES **6**

  5 MIN

 20 MIN

12 lean pork sausages
low-calorie oil spray
2 onions, sliced into rings
400g mashed potato, to
  serve
350g cooked peas, to serve

Gravy
500ml hot beef stock
3 tbsp gravy powder mixed
  with 2 tbsp water
1 tbsp Worcestershire sauce
1 tsp onion granules
1 tsp dried oregano
1 tsp tomato purée
1 tsp garlic purée
salt and pepper, to taste

1 Add the sausages to the air fryer, spray with oil spray and air-fry at 200°C for 12–14 minutes, adding in the onions after the sausages have been in for 5 minutes.

2 While they cook, whisk together all the gravy ingredients in a bowl and set aside until needed.

3 Once the sausages are cooked, add in your gravy mixture and air-fry for a further 5 minutes.

4 Serve the sausages and onion gravy with your mash and peas.

TIP
—

I love using posh ready-made mash to save myself the faff of making my own.

YORKSHIRE PUDDING STEAK WRAP

PER SERVING
569
CALORIES

My nana used to make Yorkshire puddings from scratch every Sunday, so it's no surprise that I love them. The best thing about this is it's essentially a Sunday roast wrap. All the best bits about a weekend roast but made quicker and easier thanks to your air fryer. Beef and horseradish is one of my favourite flavour pairings, but you can of course change this up depending on what leftover cooked meat you've got to hand. Chicken and stuffing, anyone?

SERVES **1**

 10 MIN

 20 MIN

low-calorie oil spray
1 egg
35g plain flour
50ml whole milk
1 tbsp horseradish sauce
1 tbsp mustard (preferably Dijon)

5 tbsp ready-made or homemade gravy
100g leftover roast beef slices or shop-bought
handful of pea shoots
salt and pepper, to taste

1   Add an 18cm round loose-bottomed tin or silicone basket liner to your air fryer and spray with the oil spray, then preheat the air fryer to 210°C for 5 minutes with the tin inside.

2   Whisk together the egg, flour and milk in a bowl to make a smooth batter. Season with salt and pepper. Add the batter to the hot tin and air-fry for 18–20 minutes.

TIP

If your cake tin doesn't fit, you can make this straight in the air fryer, using the bottom of the basket.

3   While the pudding is cooking, mix together the horseradish and mustard in a small bowl. Warm the gravy.

4   Remove the Yorkshire pudding from the air fryer, add the horseradish and mustard sauce, beef, gravy and pea shoots into the middle of the pudding, roll up and get stuck in.

CACIO E PEPE-STYLE GNOCCHI & CHICKPEAS

PER SERVING
471
CALORIES

Cacio e pepe is an ancient pasta recipe made with lots of butter, Parmesan and black pepper. Every time I have it, it just instantly transports me to my travels in Rome. Here I've borrowed these flavours to create this gorgeous air-fried gnocchi dish made that little bit more nutritious with the addition of chickpeas. If you're not veggie then you don't have to worry about finding vegetarian Parmesan, just use the stuff you usually buy in the supermarket.

SERVES **4**

 5 MIN

 20 MIN

500g gnocchi
low-calorie oil spray
1 onion, finely chopped
1 celery stick, finely chopped
400g tin of chickpeas, drained and rinsed
1 garlic clove, grated
250ml hot chicken or veggie stock

1 tbsp white wine vinegar
50g butter
75g grated vegetarian Parmesan
1 tbsp soft cream cheese
2 tsp coarsely ground black pepper, plus extra to serve
handful of fresh basil leaves

1   Add the gnocchi to the air fryer and spray with the oil spray, then air-fry for 8 minutes at 200°C. Add the chopped onion and celery, then cook for a further 4 minutes.

2   Add all the remaining ingredients, except the basil, give it a good stir and air-fry at 200°C for a further 5 minutes, stirring halfway through.

3   Scatter over the basil leaves and serve with extra black pepper, if you like.

QUICK COMFORT

CREAMY CHICKEN BAKE

EACH
494
CALORIES

This recipe is inspired by one of my favourite high-street pastry shops – the one you go to when you just want some comfort food – you know the one... Traditionally made with double cream and requiring you to cook the chicken before baking, this is an easier, lighter version that makes use of the humble tin of chicken soup. That might sound strange but just trust me on this one.

MAKES **6**

15
MIN

15
MIN

400g tin of chicken soup

80g cooked chicken, cut into small chunks

1 tsp cornflour

1 tsp dried oregano

40g light mozzarella, roughly chopped

1 tbsp soft cream cheese

2 x 320g ready-rolled puff pastry sheets

1 egg, beaten

salt and pepper, to taste

1   In a bowl, combine the soup, cooked chicken, cornflour and oregano, and microwave for 1½ minutes. Stir in the mozzarella and cream cheese. Season, to taste.

2   Cut each puff pastry sheet into six even-sized rectangles, so you have twelve in total. Spoon the chicken mixture onto six of the pastry rectangles, brush the edges with beaten egg, then cover with one of the untopped pastry rectangles and press down with a fork to seal. Score the top of each a couple of times with a knife and brush the pastry tops with more egg. Chill for 5 minutes in the fridge if you have time.

3   Line the air fryer trays with strips of baking paper to ease removal. Place the pastries in the air fryer, working in batches if necessary, and air-fry at 200°C for 15 minutes.

4   Once cooked, allow the pastries to cool slightly before removing and serving.

S'MORES DIP
with Banana & Chocolate Swirls

PER SERVING
457
CALORIES

This is chocolate heaven – chocolate and banana crêpe bites served with an unbeatable marshmallow and chocolate dip. While dipping the rolled banana crêpe into the smores dip is a very special moment, don't stop there! If you are entertaining friends and want to take it up a gear, feel free to add digestive biscuits, rich teas or fruit sticks. It's filthy and so moreish, but very comforting on a cold night with a movie.

SERVES **6**

 10 MIN

 15 MIN

2 ready-made crêpes or tortilla wraps
2 heaped tbsp chocolate hazelnut spread (I use Nutella)
2 bananas
icing sugar, to dust

Smores dip
300g milk chocolate, broken into pieces
200g large marshmallows

1   Spread each crêpe or wrap with the chocolate hazelnut spread and add a peeled banana on top of each one, placed up to the edge, then roll up the crêpe or wrap until you reach the end. Dust with icing sugar and cut into bite-size chunks. If you want, cook in the air fryer at 200°C for 7 minutes.

2   For the smores dip, place the chocolate on the bottom of a heatproof dish, then scatter the marshmallows on top in an even layer, making sure they fully cover the chocolate. Air-fry at 160°C for 5–6 minutes until gooey and melted.

3   Serve the banana swirls along with the smores dip, get stuck in and enjoy. I like to dust the crêpe bites again with icing sugar just before dipping.

TIP

This is great if you have a two-drawer air fryer, as you can get the bites and dip going at the same time.

BREEZY

BRUNCH

&

LUNCH

SWEET CHILLI PRAWN COCKTAIL PITTA

This is one of my favourite work-from-home lunches that you can turn around in a heartbeat. The flavour of the sweet chilli mayo sauce is something else, and those crispy pitta pockets soak it all up to make this really comforting. If you like things extra spicy, you can drizzle a little chilli oil over the top for added punch. Get creative with the mayo, try adding chopped gherkins or even a dash of pickle juice from the jar.

SERVES **2**

 10 MIN

 10 MIN

170g raw, peeled prawns
½ tsp paprika
2 pitta breads
salt and pepper, to taste

Sauce
2 tsp Dijon mustard
4 tbsp light mayo
2 tbsp sweet chilli sauce

1 tsp Worcestershire sauce
juice of ½ lemon
1 tsp paprika

To serve
cucumber slices
shredded lettuce
chopped chives
½ tsp chilli oil per pitta (optional)

1   Coat the prawns in the paprika and some salt and pepper, then air-fry for 5–7 minutes at 180°C until they turn pink.

2   Mix together all the sauce ingredients in a bowl.

3   Around 2 minutes before the prawns are ready, cut the pittas in half across the middle to create pockets, then air-fry for 2 minutes so they give a warm and crunchy welcome to the prawns.

4   Toss the cooked prawns in the sauce and assemble your pittas with the prawns, cucumber and lettuce, then garnish with chopped chives and a splash of chilli oil, if you like.

HOMEMADE HASH BROWN & BACON BUTTIES

EACH
573
CALORIES

Making your own hash browns when you can so easily buy frozen versions might seem unnecessary faff, but trust me when I say that these air-fried versions are just as delicious and way better for you. Paired with bacon in a butty, this is an amazing brunch, especially if you might have been out a bit too late the night before. Swap the bacon for a fried egg if you're after a veggie version.

MAKES **4**

 5 MIN

 25 MIN

4 medium Maris Piper or
  Russet potatoes
40g butter, melted
8–12 rashers of smoked
  streaky bacon

4 bread rolls, halved
salt and pepper, to taste
fried eggs and brown sauce,
  to serve (optional)

1   Boil the potatoes, skin on, in a pan of salted water for 8–10 minutes. Allow to cool, then grate into a bowl. Season well and stir in the melted butter.

2   Shape into eight small hash browns or four large ones. Air-fry for 12–15 minutes at 200°C until they are super crispy, and ideally turn them over after 10 minutes.

3   Add the bacon to the air fryer basket for the last 8 minutes – I have two drawers so I cook it in the spare one.

SERVING NOTE

Adding baked beans to this breakfast bap will take it to another level.

4   Toast the bread rolls and then top each with one or two hash browns and some bacon rashers, and a fried egg and some brown sauce, if using.

HUEVOS RANCHEROS

This is a take on the amazing classic Mexican breakfast dish, huevos rancheros. It delivers flavour on so many levels – runny fried eggs with added chorizo, avocado, feta and chilli served on a crispy tortilla with beans. This is all I could want in a brunch, it's so filling and will impress any guests you have staying over. This is traditionally served in the morning, but it works just as well at lunch or dinner time.

SERVES **3**

 10 MIN

 10 MIN

400g tin of black beans, drained, or refried beans
½ tsp ground cumin
juice of 1 lime
6 tbsp tomato purée
6 mini tortilla wraps
3 eggs
30g chorizo, crumbled
salt and pepper, to taste

To garnish
hot sauce of your choice
tomato salsa
30g feta cheese, crumbled
handful of fresh coriander
½ ripe avocado, diced
1 lime, cut into wedges

1   In a bowl, combine the beans, cumin, lime juice, 2 tablespoons of the tomato purée and some salt and pepper.

2   Spread the remaining tomato purée over three of the tortilla wraps, then top each with the remaining three tortillas. (This helps the tortillas stay flat and not curl upwards during cooking.)

3   Spread the bean mixture evenly over the top tortillas, leaving room for an egg in the middle. Crack an egg into each hole and sprinkle over the chorizo. Air-fry for 7–8 minutes at 190°C.

4   Finish with the garnishes and enjoy the flavour bomb.

CHEESE, EGG & SPINACH BOATS

PER SERVING
530
CALORIES

This is a dish based on Kachapuri, a traditional Georgian dish, which is basically cheese-filled bread in the shape of a boat. It's an absolutely world-class combo and I urge you to order it next time you see it if you've never tried it before. My version involves puff pastry as you can buy it ready-made instead of having to make bread dough. These are moreish but very filling, so I find one split between two is enough if you're having these for breakfast.

SERVES 4

10 MIN

20 MIN

320g ready-rolled puff pastry sheet
200g baby spinach
75g feta cheese, chopped
75g light mozzarella, chopped
juice of 1 lemon

1 tbsp dill, chopped
½ tsp chilli flakes
2 tbsp butter, melted
3 eggs, 1 beaten
sesame seeds, for sprinkling
salt and pepper, to taste

1   Cut the pastry in half lengthways, then turn in the edges of both in one small roll to create a rim. Pinch the bottom of each pastry piece hard so it creates almost a boat shape.

2   Wilt the spinach in a pan, then squeeze to remove the excess water. Transfer the spinach to a large bowl and mix with the feta, mozzarella, lemon juice, dill, chilli flakes, some salt and pepper, and the melted butter. Fill the inside of those lil' boats with this mixture. Brush the rims with the beaten egg, sprinkle with sesame seeds and air-fry for 12 minutes at 190°C.

3   Open the drawer and make a little well in the centre of the filling in each boat, crack an egg into each and air-fry again for a further 6 minutes at the same temperature. Serve hot and enjoy.

GREEK SALAD TORTILLA EGG BOWL

PER SERVING
785
CALORIES

Anything that resembles Greek food or flavour in any shape or form and I am there, all over it. This is a quick and easy lunch recipe that you can rustle up in no time and reap the rewards, with a crunchy tortilla filled with cheese, olives, tomatoes and egg. Lunchtime can't get any easier than this.

SERVES **1**

 10 MIN

 15 MIN

2 eggs
¼ red onion, diced
100g cherry tomatoes, chopped
1 tsp dried oregano
50g feta cheese, crumbled
50g pitted green olives, chopped

handful of fresh basil, chopped
1 large or 2 small tortilla wraps
salt and pepper, to taste
fresh dill sprigs, to garnish
drizzle of extra virgin olive oil, to garnish (optional)

1   In a bowl, beat the eggs, then add in all the other ingredients, apart from the tortilla(s) and garnishes. Season with salt and pepper.

2   Remove the tray from the air fryer basket and line it with the tortilla(s) to form a shallow boat/bowl. Carefully pour the egg mix into the tortilla bowl and then air-fry for 13–14 minutes at 180°C.

3   Allow to cool for 2–3 minutes before using a fish slice or spatula to carefully remove the tortilla and place it onto a board or plate.

4   Garnish with dill sprigs and a drizzle of olive oil, if you like, and enjoy.

TIP
—

To save on washing-up, line a heatproof bowl or shallow dish with the tortillas, instead of assembling directly in the air fryer basket.

CHEESE & STUFFING FILLED TOMATOES

EACH
214
CALORIES

This might sound like a strange combo, but picture this: roasted tomatoes filled with cheese, breadcrumbs, garlic and fresh herbs. Trust me, we are on to a winner here. You can serve this with a simple salad for lunch, but my favourite thing is to let each tomato fall apart a bit and then spread it all on bread with a drizzle of oil, balsamic and more fresh basil. Total comfort food.

MAKES **6**

 10 MIN

 10 MIN

6 large tomatoes
4 garlic cloves, peeled
handful of fresh basil leaves,
    plus extra to garnish
2 tbsp pine nuts

170g fresh breadcrumbs
80g feta cheese
drizzle of olive oil
2 tbsp balsamic glaze
salt and pepper, to taste

1   Slice off the top of the tomatoes to create lids. Scoop out the insides and add the flesh to a food processor with the garlic cloves, the handful of fresh basil, the pine nuts and some seasoning. Blitz until nearly smooth.

2   Add the breadcrumbs and the feta, and blitz briefly.

3   Remove the mixture from the processor bowl and fill the tomatoes with it.

4   Pop the tomato lids on, drizzle with olive oil and air-fry for 10 minutes at 200°C.

5   Once cooked, drizzle the stuffed tomatoes with the balsamic glaze and garnish with basil leaves.

SPICED SALMON POKE BOWL & WASABI MAYO

PER SERVING
862
CALORIES

Poke bowls are so many people's go-to working lunch option and here is a speedy version you can make yourself. The crunch from the gorgeous veg brings such a nice freshness to a very comforting bowl of rice. Wasabi isn't the easiest ingredient to find, and not everyone likes its heat, so you can use your favourite shop-bought spicy mayo in any colour or spice level you like instead.

SERVES **4**

15 MIN

15 MIN

4 skinless salmon fillets,
    cut into cubes
280g sushi rice
100g edamame beans
4 carrots, grated
1 cucumber, sliced
1 avocado, sliced

Salmon coating
1 tbsp vegetable oil
1 tbsp honey
1 tsp garlic powder

1 tsp paprika
2 tbsp mild chilli powder

Wasabi mayo
½ tbsp wasabi paste
6 tbsp light mayo
juice of 1 lime

To garnish
1 tbsp sesame seeds
2 spring onions, sliced
drizzle of soy sauce

1   Mix the salmon cubes with the coating ingredients and air-fry for 12 minutes at 190°C. If you have time to leave the salmon to marinate for 5 minutes, it will have a more flavoursome end result.

2   Meanwhile, cook the rice until sticky and gorgeous. You can also cook the rice in advance, let it cool completely, then refrigerate until needed and serve cold. Combine all the wasabi mayo ingredients in a bowl.

3   Divide the rice between four bowls, then top each with the cooked salmon, the veg and the wasabi mayo. Garnish with the sesame seeds, spring onions and a drizzle of soy sauce.

HAWAIIAN CALZONE TORTILLA PIZZA

EACH
455
CALORIES

Ham and pineapple pizza is one of those love it or hate it things – it can get so controversial! Personally, I'm a fan and love the combo of ham, pineapple and cheese. I've used wraps here instead of pizza bases because it makes them a little lighter, but you can easily swap them out if you prefer. You could also buy or make your own flatbreads.

MAKES **2**

 10 MIN

 10 MIN

2 tortilla wraps
100g passata or 4 tbsp tomato purée mixed with 1 tbsp barbecue sauce
4 slices of cooked ham, chopped into small chunks
40g pineapple, chopped (fresh or tinned)

100g mozzarella (I use reduced fat), chopped into small cubes
1 tsp dried oregano
1 egg, beaten
salt and pepper, to taste
handful of basil leaves, to garnish

1   Place the wraps on a chopping board and spread the passata or tomato/barbecue sauce mix over each. Add the ham, pineapple and mozzarella to the wraps. Sprinkle over the oregano and season with salt and pepper.

2   Brush the outer rim of each wrap with beaten egg and then fold over each wrap, pressing with a fork to seal it. Brush the outside of each calzone with beaten egg and air-fry at 200°C for 10 minutes.

3   Garnish with the basil leaves and serve.

SERVING NOTE

These are perfect served with a garlic mayo or barbecue sauce on the side for dipping.

ZINGY CHICKEN WRAP

PER SERVING
678
CALORIES

Chicken wraps make such a good lunch, and this air-fried version is going to become your new go-to. Based on one of my favourite fast food chain chicken wraps, this is a healthier version, which lets the air fryer do the work instead of the deep-fat fryer. The cornflake coating makes the chicken extra crispy but I love using chilli nachos instead for a bit of extra flavour.

SERVES **2**

  10 MIN

 15 MIN

1 egg
100g cornflakes, or chilli nachos for heat, crushed
2 chicken breasts, cut into cubes
low-calorie oil spray
2 tortilla wraps
handful of cherry tomatoes, chopped
shredded iceberg lettuce

Dressing
4 tbsp light mayo
1 garlic clove, minced
juice of ½ lemon
salt and pepper, to taste

1   Add the egg and the cornflakes or nachos to two separate bowls. Dip the chicken into the egg first, shaking off any excess, then into the cornflakes/nachos to evenly coat. Spray the coated chicken with the oil spray and air-fry for 12 minutes at 200°C.

2   Combine all the dressing ingredients in a small bowl.

3   If you have a gas hob, give your tortilla wraps just a slight char over it, or you can just eat the wraps cold. Lay the tortillas on a board and fill with the chicken, dressing, tomatoes and lettuce. Roll them up, then pop back into the air fryer for 1 final minute, if you like. Perfection!

CHICKEN BANH MI

PER SERVING
765
CALORIES

An air fryer truly brings stale bread back to life with just a drizzle of water and a quick blast of heat. So here is one of my favourite street food recipes to jazz up your sarnie. It has a phenomenal flavour and is so simple to make. You can play around with the fillings but whatever way you change it you won't be disappointed. You can also use cooked meats or tuna to save even more time.

SERVES **2**

 15 MIN

 15 MIN

200g boneless and skinless chicken thighs, left whole
1 large stale baguette, halved to make two rolls, or 2 smaller half baguettes
1 cucumber, sliced
1 carrot, julienned or grated
handful of fresh coriander
1 red chilli, sliced, to garnish

Marinade
juice of 1 lemon
1 tsp Chinese 5 spice
1 tbsp dark soy sauce
1 tsp sesame oil
1 tbsp honey
salt and pepper, to taste

Dressing
1 tsp soy sauce
1 tbsp honey
1 tsp sweet chilli sauce
1 tsp sriracha
2 tbsp light mayo

1   Combine all the marinade ingredients in a bowl, then toss in the chicken thighs to coat well. If you've got time, you could transfer this to a plastic tub or ziplock bag and leave to marinate overnight or for a few hours in the fridge.

2   Air-fry the chicken for 12–14 minutes at 200°C. Add the stale bread for the last 3–4 minutes. Slice the cooked chicken.

3   Combine all the ingredients for the dressing in a bowl.

4   When the chicken is ready, cut open the rolls, then fill with the cooked chicken, the cucumber slices, carrot and coriander before drizzling over the dressing and garnishing with the chilli.

GARLIC-CRUMBED SALMON & WHIPPED SOFT CHEESE

PER SERVING
444
CALORIES

I am obsessed with salmon cooked in the air fryer, and this version with a garlic breadcrumb coating is no exception. I first tried this with lamb, then found that it works perfectly with salmon. Paired with a gorgeous whipped cream cheese and salad, it honestly will send your tastebuds into overdrive.

SERVES **4**

 15 MIN

 15 MIN

SERVING NOTE

Serve with your favourite salad. I like a simple mix of capers, radishes, chickpeas, rocket and toasted pumpkin seeds.

4 salmon fillets (I prefer without the skin)
2 tbsp Dijon mustard
low-calorie oil spray

Crumb
2 slices of stale sourdough
zest of 1 lime
zest of ½ lemon
1 garlic clove, grated
handful of fresh parsley

small handful of fresh chives
1 tsp dried basil

Whipped cheese
200g cottage or cream cheese
juice of 1 lemon
1 garlic clove, grated
handful of fresh parsley
1 tsp caper brine
salt and pepper, to taste

1   Blitz all the crumb ingredients in a food processor to a rough crumb.

2   Coat the top of each salmon fillet with the Dijon mustard, then press in the crumb well. Spray with the oil spray and then air-fry for 11–12 minutes at 200°C.

3   While the salmon is cooking, whip or blitz the cottage/cream cheese and all the other ingredients in a clean food processor until smooth.

4   Plate up the salmon with the whipped cheese alongside, with salad or sides of your choice, and enjoy.

CANDIED BACON & CHEESE PASTRY

Upside-down puff pastry tarts have gone viral recently and for good reason. They're so easy, so filling and the pastry comes out extra crispy. I've used bacon and cheese here with a bit of added sweetness from the honey because who doesn't love that combo, but I urge you to play around with this technique – there are so many great versions out there.

MAKES **4**

 5 MIN

 10 MIN

320g ready-rolled puff pastry sheet
4 tbsp honey, or as needed
8 rashers of smoked streaky bacon

80g Cheddar cheese, grated
1 egg, beaten

1   Unroll the puff pastry and slice into 4 rectangles. Set aside.

2   Add the honey to four strips of baking paper, each just smaller than the size of a puff pastry rectangle, and spread it out with a spoon.

3   Lay two rashers of bacon over each spread of honey, sprinkle over the cheese, then top with a rectangle of pastry. Brush with the beaten egg.

4   Transfer the pastries to the air fryer, working in batches if needed, and air-fry at 200°C for 10 minutes. To make the bacon extra crisp, flip the pastries and cook for a further 2 minutes and reglaze with more honey, if required.

CHOCOLATE CHURRO-STYLE BAKED OATS

While not actually involving any dough, this oat-based pudding with an oozing chocolate centre and cinnamon and sugar topping gives me serious churro vibes. I use Nutella here because I'm not sure I can think of anything better than the flavours of churro mixed with oozing chocolate spread, but you could switch this up for Biscoff or even jam.

SERVES **2**

15
MIN

15
MIN

60g porridge oats
160g Greek yogurt
1 heaped tsp cocoa powder
½ tsp baking powder
1 tbsp granulated sweetener
1 tsp vanilla extract
4 tbsp milk
1 egg

½ tsp butter
1 tbsp chocolate hazelnut
    spread (I use Nutella)

To top
½ tsp ground cinnamon
½ tsp brown sugar

1   Blitz the oats in a food processor until you get the texture of rough flour. You don't have to do this step, but it gives a much better result.

2   Mix the oats in a bowl with all the other ingredients, except the butter and Nutella. Preheat the air fryer to 180°C.

TIP
—

You'll need two ramekins for this recipe. If you don't have any, two small heatproof bowls would work as well.

3   Grease the ramekins of choice with the butter and then divide half the oat mixture between them. Add in the Nutella and then top with the remaining oat mixture, ensuring the chocolate spread is covered.

4   Scatter the cinnamon and brown sugar over the puddings and air-fry for 12–15 minutes. Check the oats after 12 minutes, as some air fryers cook quicker than others. Tuck in and enjoy.

STRAWBERRY TOASTS
with Whipped Ricotta & a Meringue Crumb

PER SERVING
448
CALORIES

I first made this dish when I was craving a pavlova and had a tonne of strawberries in the fridge. The result is this Eton mess-style strawberry toast. If that sounds weird to you, just trust me. I am very aware the only thing we are air-frying here is the bread with some butter and cinnamon, but I had to include this recipe – it's absolute brunch heaven.

SERVES **4**

 15 MIN

 5 MIN

200g strawberries, cut in half
1 tbsp sugar
juice of 1 lemon
butter, ideally half-fat, for spreading
4 thick slices of brioche bread
1 tsp ground cinnamon
1 meringue, crumbled

fresh mint leaves, to garnish
drizzle of honey, to serve (optional)

Ricotta mix
250g ricotta cheese
100g Greek yogurt
1 tsp vanilla extract
2 heaped tbsp icing sugar

1   In a bowl, toss the strawberries in the sugar and lemon juice, then set aside.

2   Butter the bread on both sides and sprinkle with the cinnamon, then air-fry at 190°C for 5 minutes.

3   Meanwhile, blitz all the ingredients for the ricotta mix in a blender, or mix together well in a bowl, until thick.

4   To assemble, spread the ricotta mix over the cinnamon toast, then top with the strawberries and crumbled meringue. Finish with the fresh mint and a drizzle of honey, if you like.

STRAWBERRY & CREAM MILLE FEUILLE

EACH
873
CALORIES

I am going to be bold and say this might be my favourite recipe in the book and it uses just five ingredients. I had strawberries and puff pastry in the fridge one day, had a play around, and was genuinely blown away by the result. This is probably not a very traditional way of making a mille feuille, but the flavours really are unbeatable. This is definitely one of the more calorific recipes in the book but, as I always say, health is all about balance.

MAKES **3**

 15 MIN

 15 MIN

320g ready-rolled puff pastry sheet
50g icing sugar
210ml double cream

70g strawberry or raspberry jam
handful of strawberries, cut in half

1   On a sheet of baking paper, cut the puff pastry sheet into nine even rectangles, then layer them on top of each other 3 x 3. So you will have three piles with three layers. Sprinkle each stack with some of the icing sugar.

2   Add the pastry stacks to the air fryer with the baking paper and air-fry at 200°C for 15 minutes.

3   Allow the pastry to cool completely, then turn the stacks onto their sides and cut into three – so you're dividing the stacks lengthways back into their three original layers.

4   Whip the double cream in a bowl with an electric whisk until thick and pipeable – you can add a pinch of icing sugar if required. Transfer to a piping bag fitted with a nozzle or use a spoon for spreading.

5   Onto the bottom and middle section of each pastry stack, pipe or spoon over the cream, spread the jam and scatter over some strawberries. Pop the remaining pastry piece on top. Dust the top with the remaining icing sugar to finish.

TIP
—
If you like, you can reduce the calories by only using two layers of pastry rather than three.

SPEEDY

SIDES

&

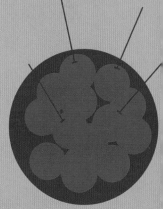

SHARING

JALAPEÑO CORNBREAD

PER SERVING
453
CALORIES

I first tried a spicy cornbread like this in a bakery in New York and knew I had to have a go at making my own version – it's just so good. The combo of the cornbread with jalapeños and cheese is out of this world and it makes such a good side to stews and soups. Put this down in the middle of the table and watch it disappear before your eyes.

SERVES **4**

 10 MIN

 20 MIN

125g plain flour
1 tsp bicarbonate of soda
125ml milk
75g Greek yogurt
1 large egg
75g butter, melted and cooled slightly

125g tinned sweetcorn, drained
75g pickled jalapeños, drained and roughly chopped
100g Cheddar cheese, grated
salt and pepper, to taste

1   Preheat the air fryer to 200°C and line a 1lb loaf tin with greasproof paper.

2   In a large bowl, combine the flour, bicarbonate of soda and a little seasoning. In another bowl, combine the milk, yogurt, egg and melted butter.

3   Add the wet ingredients to the dry, then stir in the sweetcorn, jalapeños and Cheddar.

4   Transfer the mix to the lined tin and air-fry for 20 minutes, covering partway through if the top starts to get too dark.

5   Once cooked, let it cool in the tin for 30 minutes on a work surface; the bread will continue to cook slightly. Cut into pieces to serve.

TIP
—

If you have a big enough air fryer, double this quantity and up the size of your tin for a larger version. Great if you're hosting friends.

AIR-FRIED BAKED CAMEMBERT

PER SERVING
220
CALORIES

A baked Camembert immediately makes me think of Christmas, but I think this works all year round and will often serve it with a salad during summer. Ready in just 12 minutes, it's the ultimate party snack and couldn't be easier. While this is a great sharing dish, it also makes a lovely indulgent starter for just two on date night.

SERVES **4**

  5 MIN

 15 MIN

1 x 250g Camembert (ideally boxed)
1 tbsp truffle oil (optional)
1 tbsp honey

1 tsp chilli flakes
1 tsp fresh thyme leaves
toasted bread, to serve

1   Remove the plastic from around the cheese and place it back in its box, lined with some foil or greaseproof paper. Drizzle the cheese with the truffle oil, if using, place it in the air fryer basket and top the cheese with the honey, chilli flakes and thyme. If your Camembert didn't come in a wooden box, place it in a heatproof ceramic dish that fits in the air fryer. Air-fry for 12 minutes at 160°C.

2   Remove from the air fryer and serve the cheese in its box as it's very delicate and special!

3   Serve with toasted bread for dipping.

TIP

Use two long strips of greaseproof paper in a cross under the cheese box to help when removing the cheese from the air fryer basket.

SPICED LAMB SAMOSAS

EACH
101
CALORIES

I love making these to serve alongside a homemade curry or even to go along with a takeaway. Packed with flavour and spice and succulent lamb mince, these are little bites of heaven and so moreish. If you wanted to make a veggie version, you could also swap out the lamb for potatoes and peas. This recipe makes 18 samosas, so plenty to go round if you have people over.

MAKES **18**

10
MIN

20
MIN

500g lean lamb mince
1 onion, finely chopped
1 tbsp ground turmeric
1 tsp paprika
1 tsp chilli powder
½ tsp ground coriander
1 tsp ground cumin
½ tsp dried mint
1 tbsp garlic purée
2 tbsp tomato purée
6 sheets of filo pastry

low-calorie oil spray
salt and pepper, to taste

Mint yogurt
150g Greek yogurt
2 tbsp mint, finely chopped
juice of ½ lemon
1 garlic clove, crushed
½ tsp freshly ground black pepper
100g pomegranate seeds, to garnish

1   Fry the lamb mince, onion, spices, dried mint and some salt and pepper over a medium-high heat for about 6 minutes. After 4 minutes, mix through the garlic and tomato purées. You could also do this stage in an air fryer preheated to 200°C for 12 minutes (add the garlic and tomato purées after 10 minutes).

2   Cut each filo sheet into three and spray with oil spray along the inside. At the bottom of each filo sheet, add some of the lamb mix, then fold over a corner diagonally, then fold again, repeating until you reach the top and the lamb mix is covered in filo numerous times.

3   Spray the outside of the samosas with oil and air-fry for 10 minutes at 180°C, turning halfway through.

4   While they cook, mix together the mint yogurt ingredients, except the pomegranate seeds, and transfer into a small serving bowl.

5   Once the samosas are cooked, cool slightly, then serve with the mint yogurt, with pomegranate seeds sprinkled over.

CRISPY SALT & PEPPER SQUID

PER SERVING
207
CALORIES

I know I'm not alone in finding it so hard to resist crispy squid if I see it on a menu. I genuinely struggle to order anything new once I know it's there. Here is a really simple version using your air fryer and paired with a fiery wasabi mayo. You can get fresh prepared squid from most supermarkets and you can also buy it frozen, which works just as well – just let it defrost before slicing. If you can't get hold of wasabi, you can serve this with garlic mayo instead.

SERVES **6**

 15 MIN

 15 MIN

600g squid, cut into strips and scored to tenderise
1 tbsp light soy sauce
1 tsp sesame oil
1 tbsp garlic purée
5 tbsp cornflour
2 tbsp plain flour
1 tsp each of salt and pepper
2 tbsp vegetable oil

1 green chilli, finely diced
1 red chilli, finely diced
1 tsp rice wine vinegar

Wasabi mayo
4 tbsp light mayo
½ tsp wasabi powder or purée

1   Pat the sliced squid dry with kitchen paper and mix with the soy sauce, sesame oil and garlic purée in a bowl.

2   Combine the cornflour, plain flour and salt and pepper in a bowl. Toss the squid in the mix to coat and preheat the air fryer to 200°C. Add the vegetable oil to the air fryer and allow to heat for 2–3 minutes before adding the squid, tossing carefully to coat, then air-fry for 8–10 minutes, turning halfway if you can. For the last 3 minutes of cooking, add the chilli and rice wine vinegar and give the basket a little shake.

3   Combine the wasabi mayo ingredients in a small bowl.

4   Serve the crispy squid with that fiery wasabi mayo. Divine!

TIP
___

If you have time, you could put the squid in the soy/sesame/garlic mix in the fridge to marinate for an hour.

JALAPEÑO POPPERS
with a Zesty Dip

PER SERVING 178 CALORIES

Jalapeño poppers are classic party food, ideal served with a cold beer with friends. I have made numerous versions of these before and, while I do change it up, these are inspired by an amazing Mob recipe, which I love. There's no chopping involved, they really couldn't be easier. It's important to preheat your air fryer here so they come out really nice and crispy.

SERVES **4**

  10 MIN

 15 MIN

12–15 whole jalapeños, fresh or pickled from a jar
olive oil, for drizzling
salt and pepper, to taste

Batter
6 tbsp plain flour
1 tbsp Cajun seasoning
100ml juice from a jar of pickles
juice of 1 lime

Dip
3 tbsp soured cream
1 tbsp coriander, chopped
juice of 1 lime
1 garlic clove, finely grated

1   Preheat your air fryer to 200°C. Meanwhile, combine the batter ingredients with some seasoning in a bowl and fully dip the jalapeños in the mixture to coat. Add to your preheated air fryer, drizzle over some olive oil and cook for 12 minutes until the batter is crisp and golden.

2   Combine all the dip ingredients in a bowl and serve alongside the crispy jalapeño poppers.

PATATAS BRAVAS

PER SERVING
284
CALORIES

These are a tapas must-have – perfect as a side or even just as another dish for guests to nibble on as finger food. This is a lower-calorie and much quicker way to make the classic dish. You'd usually expect the potatoes to be cubed, but a restaurant I visited in Malaga used whole baby potatoes, and I haven't looked back since.

SERVES **4**

 10 MIN

 20 MIN

800g small waxy potatoes, skin on, halved or left whole
1 tbsp olive oil
3 tbsp light mayo
2 garlic cloves, crushed
fresh parsley, chopped, to garnish

Tomato sauce
1 tbsp olive oil
½ onion, finely diced
400g tin of chopped tomatoes
½ tsp salt
pinch of caster sugar
1 tsp hot or sweet smoked paprika
1 tsp sherry vinegar (or red wine vinegar)

1   Coat the potatoes in the oil, then air-fry at 200°C for 18–20 minutes, shaking halfway through cooking.

2   While the potatoes are cooking, heat the oil for the tomato sauce in a small saucepan and fry the onion over a low heat for 4–5 minutes, or until soft. Add in the tinned tomatoes, salt, sugar and paprika. Stir well and allow to simmer for 10 minutes. Once cooked, add the vinegar and mix well. Set aside until serving.

3   Mix together the mayo and the garlic and set aside.

4   Once the potatoes are cooked, transfer to a serving bowl and top with the tomato sauce and then the garlic mayo. Scatter over some chopped fresh parsley and – done!

EASY FILTHY FRIES

PER SERVING
400
CALORIES

In my first air fryer book, I included a recipe for chips that were made from scratch, but here I am cheating by using frozen chips to make these loaded fries. It's a great shortcut if you're in a bit of a rush and it's perfectly okay to reach into the freezer on those days when you don't have quite as much energy. It's also worth noting that air-fried frozen chips taste phenomenal, even more so when paired with a chorizo crumb, sour cream and hot sauce.

SERVES **4**

 10 MIN

 20 MIN

500g frozen chips (thin-cut will take less time, naturally)
low-calorie oil spray
1 tbsp Cajun seasoning
80g soft chorizo, crumbled (or you can use bacon bits)
1 tbsp half-fat butter
2 garlic cloves, minced

2 tbsp grated Parmesan
4 tbsp soured cream
4 tbsp green chilli/jalapeño hot sauce or your hot sauce of choice
small handful of fresh chives, chopped
handful of pickled red onions

1   Spray your chips with the oil spray in the air fryer basket and sprinkle over the Cajun seasoning, giving them a good shake to coat. Air-fry for 12 minutes at 200°C for thin chips and 15–20 minutes for thick-cut.

2   Around 5 minutes before the chips are ready, toss in the crumbled chorizo or bacon bits.

3   Meanwhile, melt the butter in the microwave on high for 1 minute with the minced garlic cloves.

4   Once the chips are cooked, toss them in the garlic butter, sprinkle over the Parmesan, then top with soured cream, hot sauce, chives and pickled red onions. Just incredible!

LOADED POTATO SKINS

PER SERVING
259
CALORIES

I will never get bored of making potatoes of each and every form in my air fryer. I am from Ireland, so when it comes to spuds I know what I'm talking about, and I love how much easier the air fryer makes it to cook wedges, chips, roasties, I could go on... This time we're going for potato skins loaded with chicken, crispy onions and all the works. This works so well as a pre-dinner snack if you're hosting, but is also a delicious lunch for two with a side salad. The potatoes can be cooked in advance and then given a quick 3 minutes in the air fryer to bring them back to life before being loaded up.

SERVES **6**

 5 MIN

 25 MIN

6 medium potatoes
low-calorie oil spray
1 tbsp paprika
200g cooked chicken,
    shredded
75g shop-bought crispy
    onions

100g soured cream
100ml hot sauce
salt and pepper, to taste
2 tbsp chives, chopped
    to garnish

1 Pierce the potatoes with a fork, then microwave on high for 12 minutes until softened. Cut them in half and scoop out half of the insides with a spoon. Spray the potato skins with oil, dust with the paprika, season with salt and pepper, and air-fry at 200°C for 10–12 minutes, turning halfway through.

2 Load up with the cooked chicken, crispy onions, a drizzle of soured cream and hot sauce, and a sprinkling of chives. Enjoy!

TIP
—

Don't let the scooped-out insides go to waste, use the leftover potato to make the fish cakes on page 48.

ONION RINGS

PER SERVING
243
CALORIES

Onion rings are one of my absolute favourite sides from the chippie. Of course, the ones you get from the chippie are battered and deep-fried, so we're being a touch healthier here. These are a lot easier to make, too, and are coated in a light crumb that's seasoned and air-fried to crispy perfection. I know these are usually served as a side, but I can confirm I have also made them just so I can eat them on their own with ketchup, salt and vinegar. But you do you.

SERVES **4**

 10 MIN

 10 MIN

100g plain flour
1 tbsp paprika
2 eggs
120g panko breadcrumbs

2 large onions, sliced into thick rings
low-calorie oil spray
salt and pepper, to taste

1   In one bowl, mix the flour, paprika and some salt and pepper, and in another bowl, beat the eggs. In a third bowl, combine the panko breadcrumbs with a little salt and pepper.

2   Dip the onion rings into the flour mixture to coat, then into the egg, shaking off any excess, then into the panko breadcrumbs to coat well. Spray well with oil and air-fry for 8–10 minutes at 200°C, ideally turning halfway and respraying with oil – don't overcrowd the basket either, or stack too many, or they won't crisp well. A slight overlapping is fine.

3   Get stuck in and enjoy.

SWEETCORN RIBS
with Feta & Spicy Almond Sauce

PER SERVING
151
CALORIES

There has been a bit of a trend for these recently and it's not hard to see why. Deceptively simple to make, they also take on flavour so well and you can serve them with all sorts of tasty sauces and toppings. I've gone with feta and a spicy almond butter sauce. While these are a great side at any time of day, I also think they work especially well as a brunch dish if you've got people round and want to make a bit of an effort.

SERVES **6**

 10 MIN

 20 MIN

4 corn on the cob
2 tbsp butter
1 tsp smoked paprika
1 tsp chilli powder
1 tsp ground cumin
½ tsp ground turmeric
juice of 1 lime
salt and pepper, to taste

Almond sauce
4 tbsp almond butter
1 tsp paprika
1 tsp chilli
juice of 1 lemon
juice of 1 lime

To garnish
2 red chillies, finely diced
fresh coriander, roughly
    chopped
40g feta cheese, crumbled

1   Microwave the corn for 5 minutes on high until slightly softened; this makes the cobs easier to cut through. Cut each cob into 4 pieces lengthways.

2   Melt the butter in the microwave, then add in the spices, lime juice and some seasoning. Glaze the corn ribs with this mix. Air-fry the sweetcorn ribs at 200°C for 15 minutes.

3   Mix all the almond sauce ingredients together in a bowl.

4   Serve topped with the garnishes and the sauce on the side.

CARAMELISED CARROTS
with Feta & Nuts

PER SERVING
206
CALORIES

These are perfect all year round, gorgeous in the summer as a salad for a barbecue, just as good during the colder months to accompany a roast with gravy. It also couldn't be easier, you don't even need to slice the carrots, provided they are thin and not too chunky.

SERVES **4**

 5 MIN

 15 MIN

500g thin carrots, or regular carrots cut into batons
1 tsp olive oil
juice of ½ lemon
1 tsp half-fat butter
1 tsp grated nutmeg

2 tbsp honey
30g hazelnuts, chopped
30g feta cheese, crumbled
2 tbsp fresh parsley, roughly chopped
salt and pepper, to taste

1   Halve any slightly larger carrots lengthways, then put them in a bowl with all the other ingredients, except the nuts, feta and parsley. Season with some salt and pepper, and toss to coat. Add to the air fryer and cook for 13–15 minutes at 190°C.

2   Top the cooked carrots with the hazelnuts, feta and parsley, and serve.

SOY, BUTTER & SESAME SPROUTS

PER SERVING
126
CALORIES

Sprouts are notoriously controversial but I am here to convince even the haters. These are buttery and sticky from the honey with a salty tang from the soy sauce – get ready for them to become one of your go-to sides. If you want the flavour to be more plain, maybe to go with your Sunday roast, you can use the same method and simply pair with butter and olive oil for a more classic version.

SERVES **6**

 5 MIN

 15 MIN

400g Brussels sprouts, trimmed
2 tbsp butter
1 tbsp dark soy sauce
1 tbsp sesame oil

2 tbsp honey
low-calorie oil spray
1 tbsp sesame seeds

1   Boil the kettle and pour the water into a heatproof bowl to cover the sprouts. Leave to steep for 5 minutes – there's no need to parboil them, just let them ever so slightly soften before putting them in the air fryer.

2   Add the sprouts to the air fryer with all the other ingredients, except the sesame seeds, spray with the oil spray and air-fry for 8–10 minutes at 200°C, shaking halfway through cooking.

3   Once cooked, toss through the sesame seeds and serve.

ROASTED RED PEPPER, TOMATO & ORZO SALAD

PER SERVING
338
CALORIES

There's nothing I could say here which would explain just how obsessed I am with this salad, it is one of my absolute favourite recipes. Full disclosure – the inspiration for this recipe came from a pre-packaged supermarket salad, you may even recognise it once you've rustled it up. This makes a great side or sharing dish, but I also love it as a pack-up-and-go lunch.

SERVES **4**

 10 MIN

 15 MIN

2 red peppers, chopped
1 red onion, chopped
120g cherry tomatoes, halved
low-calorie oil spray
1 tsp paprika
1 tsp dried oregano
300g orzo
handful of sundried
   tomatoes, chopped
salt and pepper, to taste
2 tbsp basil, chopped,
   to garnish

Dressing
70ml red wine vinegar or
   balsamic vinegar
handful of fresh basil,
   chopped
1 tbsp olive oil
2 garlic cloves, grated
1 tsp dried oregano
juice of 1 lemon

1   Spray the red peppers, onion and cherry tomatoes with the oil in the air fryer basket, then scatter over the paprika, oregano and some salt and pepper. Air-fry for 12–14 minutes at 180°C.

2   While the veg is in the air fryer, cook your orzo – you can also cook this in advance and refrigerate. Combine all the dressing ingredients in a bowl.

3   In a large bowl, toss together the roast veg, orzo, dressing and sundried tomatoes, then sprinkle over the basil to garnish, and serve.

CAULIFLOWER CHEESE

PER SERVING
378
CALORIES

Truth be told, I am not a diehard cauliflower cheese fan. It's something my mum made for us when we were younger and I used to poke it to the side of the plate. I will eat it now, but it still wouldn't be my side of choice. However, I know what a popular side it is, so I came up with this air-fried version, which has gone down very well with the cauliflower cheese lovers in my life.

SERVES **4**

 10 MIN

 20 MIN

1 large cauliflower
100g half-fat butter
1 onion, chopped
1 leek, sliced
1 garlic clove, grated
450ml skimmed milk

3 tbsp plain flour
1 tbsp Dijon mustard
100g reduced-fat Cheddar
  cheese, grated
2 tbsp fresh breadcrumbs
salt and pepper, to taste

1   Cut your cauliflower into florets and boil in a pan of lightly salted water over a medium heat for 5 minutes. Drain and add the cauliflower to an ovenproof dish in your air fryer or add directly to your air fryer basket, lined with a silicone liner.

2   Cook the butter, onion, leek and garlic in a pan over a low heat for 2 minutes until softened. Stir in the milk, flour, mustard and three-quarters of the cheese. Season with salt and pepper. Cook and stir until thick.

3   Add the sauce to the cauliflower, allowing the florets to poke through the sauce, then sprinkle over the breadcrumbs and the remaining cheese. Air-fry for 8–10 minutes at 190°C, or until crispy and golden, then serve.

HOSTING

IN

A

HURRY

BATCH-PREP BREAKFAST BAGELS

EACH
495
CALORIES

Now, while these are a perfect breakfast to serve when you have visitors or family staying over, these are also a great batch cook recipe to help you get ahead on a busy day. Prep and fill the bagels, then freeze ready to be toasted when you want them.

MAKES **6**

 5 MIN

 25 MIN

TIP
—

If you want to prep ahead, wrap the filled bagels in foil once they're cooked, then freeze. Transfer to the fridge to defrost overnight, then reheat in the air fryer for 7 minutes at 200°C.

8 bacon medallions
6 frozen hash browns
50g Cheddar cheese, grated
handful of fresh basil, chopped
6 sundried tomatoes, finely sliced
10 eggs

1 onion, finely chopped
handful of spring onions, finely chopped
2 tbsp milk
6 bagels, sliced in half
6 slices of Cheddar cheese (optional)
salt and pepper, to taste

1   Air-fry the bacon and hash browns for 8–10 minutes at 200°C – after 10 minutes the bacon will be very crispy, so you might prefer to take it out after 8 minutes.

2   While these are cooking, prep the rest of your ingredients.

3   Cut up the bacon and hash browns into small pieces and mix together in a bowl with the grated cheese, basil, sundried tomatoes, eggs, onion, spring onions, milk and some salt and pepper.

4   Remove the tray and add the mix to the air fryer basket, then air-fry for 12–14 minutes, or until set (cover with foil if the top is getting too dark). Cut into 6 slices and then fill the bagels with them.

5   Top each with a slice of cheese, if using, and serve.

BEETROOT & GOAT'S CHEESE TARTS

EACH
231
CALORIES

These are just gorgeous and so easy to make with ready-rolled puff pastry. Making little individual tarts like this in a muffin tray makes them ideal for a snacky starter if you've got people round, but this also makes a great midweek lunch as one large rectangular tart (you'd probably need to cook this in the oven, though). You don't technically need the muffin tray here, so if you don't have one, you can just add the tarts directly onto a piece of baking paper in the air fryer drawer.

MAKES **6**

 15 MIN

 10 MIN

320g ready-rolled puff pastry sheet
low-calorie oil spray
250g cooked beetroot, diced
50g goat's cheese, crumbled
6 tsp honey

6 tsp caramelised onion chutney
1 egg, beaten
rocket leaves, to garnish (optional)
pomegranate seeds, to garnish (optional)

1 Cut your pastry into six 10cm squares or circles using a sharp knife, a pastry cutter or by scoring around a mug with a knife. Add these to a 6-hole muffin tray greased with oil spray.

2 Preheat the air fryer to 180°C. Fill the pastry cases with the beetroot, goat's cheese and 1 teaspoon each of honey and chutney per tart – don't overfill your tarts. Brush the pastry with beaten egg anywhere that is exposed outside of the muffin tray, then add the tarts to your preheated air fryer and cook for 10 minutes.

3 Garnish with rocket and pomegranate seeds for some extra sweetness, if you like, and enjoy.

SHREDDED ROTISSERIE GARLIC CHICKEN OPEN SANDWICH

PER SERVING 404 CALORIES

Creamy garlic mayo chicken on top of crispy sourdough just screams summer to me – sitting outside in the garden, sprinklers on, birds chirping, and those beautiful sounds being drowned out by the crunch of this open sandwich. Heaven. It's not exclusive to summer, though, so please enjoy this all year round.

SERVES **6**

  10 MIN

  5 MIN

6 thick slices of sourdough bread
butter, for spreading
1 garlic clove, cut in half
600g shredded, cooked chicken

Sauce
8 tbsp light mayo
4 tbsp fat-free Greek yogurt
1 tbsp Dijon mustard

juice of 1 lemon
4 garlic cloves, minced or grated
1 tbsp capers, chopped
salt and pepper, to taste

To garnish
fresh chives, chopped
fresh dill, chopped
sliced radishes
lemon zest (optional)

1   Butter the sourdough slices and air-fry at 180°C for 5 minutes.

2   While the bread is air-frying, mix the sauce ingredients together in a bowl.

3   When the bread is crispy and ready, rub a garlic half, cut-side down, over each slice, then top with the sauce, chicken and your preferred garnishes.

LAZY LOADED NACHOS

PER SERVING
663
CALORIES

No matter how many fancy snacks you put out at a party, the star of the show will always be warm, cheesy, loaded nachos and these are made even better with extra pepperoni and jalapeños for a spicy kick. This is perfect when you're hosting because you can load up both air fryer drawers in advance, then just turn the machine on when your guests arrive. You can of course leave out the pepperoni if you want to make these veggie.

SERVES **8**

 5 MIN

 10 MIN

800g nachos
400g pizza sauce
1 tsp dried oregano
1 tsp dried basil
160g light mozzarella, grated

150g pepperoni slices
salt and pepper, to taste
200g sweet peppadew
   peppers from a jar,
   to garnish
sliced pickled jalapeños,
   to garnish

1   Add baking paper to the bottom of the air fryer so you can easily lift out the loaded nachos after cooking. Tip in the nachos.

2   In a bowl, mix the pizza sauce, herbs and some salt and pepper and pour over the top of the nachos. Sprinkle over half the cheese, then lay over the pepperoni slices followed by the rest of the cheese. Air-fry at 190°C for 7–8 minutes.

3   Serve piping hot, sprinkled with the peppadew peppers and pickled jalapeños.

CRISPY FRIED SUSHI SQUARES
with Spicy Salmon

PER SERVING
226
CALORIES

I had some leftover sushi rice one day and was inspired to make a version of this amazing crispy, spicy tuna canapé I'd had once at a restaurant in London. The result was these sushi squares and I can't actually explain how incredible they are. Crunchy rice, topped with spicy salmon and crispy onions – yes please. This recipe makes roughly 12–14 squares, but you can cut them into whatever size you like.

SERVES **6**

 20 MIN

 10 MIN

300g cooked and cooled
   sushi rice
low-calorie oil spray
200g cooked salmon, flaked
2 tbsp soy sauce
4 tbsp sriracha
2 tbsp light mayo

To garnish
sliced green chilli
50g shop-bought crispy
   onions
1 tsp sesame seeds (optional)

1   Line the bottom of a loaf tin with cling film and add the sushi rice, compacting it so it's in a layer about 5cm deep. If you can fill a few loaf tins or a larger tray, then perfect. Press it down evenly and leave in the fridge for 5 minutes.

2   Once chilled, cut it into small squares. Add the rice squares to the air fryer drawer lined with baking paper, spray with oil and air-fry for 10 minutes at 200°C. If you like, turn them over halfway through cooking.

3   Mix the salmon, soy sauce, sriracha and mayo in a bowl. Spoon this on top of the cooked rice, then garnish with green chilli slices, crispy onions and sesame seeds, if using.

TIP
—
You can start this the night before and leave the rice in the fridge overnight to really firm up, if you want.

ROASTED RED PEPPER & TOMATO SOUP

PER SERVING
338
CALORIES

I make a lot of soups in the slow cooker but did you know you can make soup in your air fryer too? This is a great one to start off a dinner with if you've got people round, but it also makes an epic batch cook recipe. If I'm having this for lunch or even a light dinner, I'll make a gorgeous cheese and mustard toastie to pull into pieces and dip into the hot soup.

SERVES **4**

 10 MIN

 20 MIN

450g tomatoes, quartered
1 tbsp olive oil
handful of sundried tomatoes, roughly chopped
3 red peppers, roughly chopped
6 garlic cloves, peeled and left whole
1 red chilli, roughly chopped
1 red onion, roughly chopped
1 tsp dried oregano

300ml hot vegetable stock
120ml single cream
handful of fresh basil, plus extra to garnish
salt and pepper, to taste

Toasties
4 slices of bread, buttered
3 tbsp Dijon mustard
8 slices of Cheddar cheese

TIP
—
If your air fryer only has one drawer, you can make your toasties under the grill.

1   For the soup, add all the ingredients to your air fryer drawer (remove the tray), except the stock, cream and basil, and cook for 20 minutes at 200°C. Combine with the hot stock, cream and basil, and either blitz everything together with a handheld blender in a pot or blitz in your air fryer drawer.

2   After the soup has been cooking for 10 minutes, start making your toasties. Spread the buttered slices of bread with mustard, top with the cheese slices, then add to the other air fryer drawer and cook at 200°C for 7 minutes until golden and the cheese has melted.

3   Serve the soup piping hot with the toastie for dipping. Garnish with some basil and a twist of black pepper.

CHICKEN, SOY & HOISIN GYOZAS

PER SERVING
252
CALORIES

Beautiful chicken gyozas, crisped in the air fryer before being lightly steamed at the end, and served with a gorgeous soy and hoisin dressing – the ultimate crowd-pleaser. The gyozas can be stuffed and sealed in advance before putting in the fridge until you're ready to cook and serve.

SERVES **6**

 20 MIN

 10 MIN

3 spring onions, finely chopped
2 tbsp soy sauce
1 tbsp ginger purée
1 tbsp garlic purée
1 tsp chilli flakes
400g chicken mince or pork mince
white pepper, to taste
30 x gyoza wrappers or wonton wrappers
low-calorie oil spray

Dressing
2 heaped tbsp hoisin sauce
1 tsp sesame oil
1 tbsp dark soy sauce

To garnish
black and white sesame seeds
2 spring onions, finely sliced

TIP
—

Gyoza wrappers can be hard to track down but you can buy them online if you can't find them. You can also buy frozen pre-made gyozas instead.

1   To make the filling, mix together the spring onions, soy, ginger, garlic, chilli flakes, mince and white pepper.

2   Add a heaped teaspoon of the filling to the centre of each gyoza wrapper, use your finger to add water to the edge, fold over and press to seal, crimping the edges. Spray with oil and air-fry for 6 minutes at 200°C.

3   Once the gyozas are cooked, add 50ml of water to the bottom of the air fryer basket. Air-fry for a further 3 minutes, or until the liquid has evaporated and the gyozas are fully cooked.

4   Combine the dressing ingredients, drizzle over the gyozas, garnish with sesame seeds and spring onions, and enjoy.

GARLIC BUTTER LOBSTER TAILS
with Chilli Linguine

PER SERVING
830
CALORIES

Lobster tails are not cheap, so this is definitely a date night or special occasion recipe. Being on a budget and saving money is so important to me; but I'm hoping all the hard work you are doing with meal prep, batch cooking and using the recipes in this book instead of ordering takeaways might leave you a little over to treat yourself to lobster tails. I serve this dish with a very simple *aglio e olio* pasta, and it is phenomenal. I also like to add a sneaky side of garlic bread and a large glass of wine – it is a date night, after all!

SERVES **2**

 15 MIN

 15 MIN

4 fresh or frozen lobster tails (defrosted, if frozen)
160g dried linguine
3 tbsp olive oil
2 garlic cloves, sliced
1 tsp chilli flakes
1 tbsp parsley, finely chopped

Garlic butter
50g butter, softened
½ tbsp parsley, finely chopped
2 garlic cloves, grated
½ tsp paprika
salt and pepper, to taste

1   If the lobster tails aren't already open, using kitchen scissors, cut along the top of them so the flesh is exposed.

2   Combine all the garlic butter ingredients in a bowl and fill the exposed insides of the lobster tails with it. Air-fry at 200°C for 8–10 minutes, or until cooked through.

3   Meanwhile, cook the pasta in a pan of boiling water until al dente. In a frying pan, heat the olive oil and gently cook the garlic slices until fragrant. Add in the chilli flakes and parsley and then toss through the hot pasta with a little seasoning.

4   Serve the lobster tails with a good helping of the linguine.

CHICKEN PAKORAS
with a Zingy Salad

PER SERVING
301
CALORIES

Chicken pakoras are a delicious Indian appetiser, with tender chicken marinated in spices before being battered and fried. There's no batter involved in this air fryer version so they feel slightly lighter. The pakoras themselves make an amazing snacky appetiser, but I also love them served with a fresh and fragrant salad. You could even serve it all in a flatbread with some yogurt.

SERVES **6**

10 MIN

20 MIN

600g boneless and skinless chicken thighs or breasts, cut into long strips
1 tbsp ginger purée
1 tbsp garlic purée
½ tsp garam masala
½ tsp ground cumin
1 tsp ground turmeric
1 tbsp paprika
2 eggs, beaten
100g cornflour
4 dashes of red food colouring
2 tbsp vegetable oil

Salad
200g pomegranate seeds
1 mango, peeled, stoned and finely chopped
handful of fresh coriander, chopped
juice of 1 lemon
juice of 1 lime
100g cherry tomatoes, chopped
1 red onion, finely chopped
salt and pepper, to taste
fresh mint leaves, to garnish

TIP
—

If you've got time, leave the coated chicken to marinate in the spices for an hour before cooking.

1   Coat the chicken in all the flavourings, then stir in the eggs, cornflour and food colouring until combined.

2   Remove the trays from the air fryer basket and preheat to 200°C for 5 minutes with the vegetable oil. Add the chicken to the air fryer and cook for 14 minutes at 200°C, turning halfway through.

3   Toss together all the ingredients for the salad in a bowl, finishing with the mint leaves.

4   Serve the chicken pakoras with the salad.

CAULIFLOWER & AUBERGINE FLATBREADS
with a Lime Yogurt

PER SERVING
372
CALORIES

One thing I can't get enough of is flatbreads, and here is a delicious veggie version. Cauliflower and aubergine are both vegetables that take on flavour incredibly well, and here they're coated in spices before going into the air fryer, then paired with zesty tahini yogurt. Simple and so satisfying. I toast my flatbreads in the air fryer, but you could also do this in a dry frying pan.

SERVES **4**

 10 MIN

 20 MIN

1 cauliflower, trimmed and cut into florets
1 aubergine, sliced
1 tbsp olive oil
1 tsp ground cumin
1 tsp ground turmeric
1 tbsp curry powder
1 tbsp paprika
1 tsp mild chilli powder
4 flatbreads
salt and pepper, to taste

fresh coriander, to garnish
pickled veg, jalapeño or red onion, to serve
hummus with a drizzle of olive oil, to serve (optional)

Yogurt
1 tbsp tahini
zest of 1 lime
6 tbsp natural yogurt

1   Coat the cauliflower florets and aubergine slices in the oil and the spices, and season to taste with salt and pepper. Air-fry for 14–16 minutes at 190°C.

2   Combine all the yogurt ingredients in a bowl.

3   Toast the flatbreads in the air fryer at 190°C for 1 minute, then top with the air-fried veg and garnish with the coriander. Serve with the yogurt, pickled veg and hummus.

POSH DOGS
with Beer-braised Onions

These always go down a treat and they remind me of the German hot dog stands at the Christmas markets that come to Belfast in the winter. Sausages served in a soft brioche roll with mustard, ketchup and beer-braised onions – who could say no to that? Get the onions going as you air-fry the sausages and everything should be ready at around the same time. You want to cook the onions slowly rather than frying them quickly so they become a soft, tangled mess at the end. However, if you don't have time, you could easily swap these out for shop-bought crispy onions for a great alternative.

SERVES **6**

 10 MIN

 20 MIN

TIP
—

Make some air-fried chips to go with these. Cook them in the air fryer at the same temperature for 12–14 minutes.

6 bratwurst-style sausages, or raw sausages of your choice
2 onions, sliced
1 tsp butter
70ml beer (the rest is for you)

1 tbsp brown sugar or honey
6 brioche finger rolls, split in half
6 tbsp American mustard
6 tbsp tomato ketchup

1   Pierce the sausages gently with a fork and air-fry for 5 minutes at 200°C. If using raw sausages, air-fry these for 12–15 minutes – they also work perfectly well.

2   In a pan, soften the onions in the butter for 5 minutes, then pour in the beer and brown sugar or honey and continue to cook gently for 12 minutes, or while the sausages are cooking.

3   Toast the finger rolls in the air fryer for the last 1 minute of the cooking time, then simply assemble by adding the sausages to the rolls, drizzling over the sauces and scattering with the onions, then you are good to go. Feeding a crowd was never so simple!

DRAGON'S BREATH CHEESY 'NDUJA & GARLIC LOAF

Like the Jalapeño Cornbread on page 131, this is another one of those great sharing breads which could be a side dish but ends up being the star of the show. Spicy from the 'nduja garlic butter and stuffed with cheese, it doesn't get much better than this. 'Nduja is pretty easy to find these days but, if you can't get any, you can substitute with chorizo mixed with a little bit of chilli powder.

SERVES **8**

 15 MIN

 10 MIN

1 large sourdough loaf
100g mozzarella (light, if you want), grated
4 tbsp sweet chilli sauce
1 red chilli, finely diced, to garnish (optional – for extra heat)
2 tbsp parsley, finely chopped

'Nduja garlic butter
100g 'nduja paste (or use 1 tsp chilli powder with 100g finely grated chorizo)
120g half-fat butter
1 heaped tsp paprika
1 tsp chilli powder
5 garlic cloves, grated
1 tbsp parsley, finely chopped
salt and pepper, to taste

1 Mix together the 'nduja garlic butter ingredients in a bowl.

2 Cut slices along the length of the sourdough – almost as if making hasselback potatoes – not cutting all the way down, and then repeat in the other direction to make a crosshatch.

3 Using about three-quarters of the butter, spread it over the inside of the slices, then fill with the mozzarella and sweet chilli sauce.

4 Melt the remaining butter in the microwave on high for 1 minute, stir, then brush it all over the outside of the loaf.

5 Air-fry for 8–10 minutes at 180°C, then garnish with the red chilli, if using, and tear apart the slices to eat.

PANTRY ESSENTIALS

Here I've included a list of some of my most-used ingredients that I try to have on hand so that I can create tasty, healthy food at home. It's not an exhaustive list and you definitely don't need to go out and buy them all at once. These are just some of the staples I aim to have in stock and recommend that you do too.

FOR FLAVOUR

- Dried herbs – in particular oregano, basil, thyme, rosemary, coriander
- Paprika, dried chilli flakes, garlic powder, onion powder, chilli powder
- Salt and pepper

FOR FAKEAWAY RECIPES

- Soy sauce, hoisin sauce, honey, rice vinegar, tins of coconut milk, sriracha, peanut butter
- Garlic and ginger – you can use fresh, dried, frozen or jars of lazy ginger/garlic

SAUCE ESSENTIALS

- Stock cubes – veg, chicken and beef
- Cornflour to help you thicken a sauce and coat your meats
- Tins of chopped tomatoes or passata
- Tomato purée
- Worcestershire sauce

TO PAIR WITH YOUR AIR-FRIED FOODS

- Rice
- Couscous
- Pasta
- Potatoes of all kinds – you can cook these in the air fryer too
- Low-calorie spray

FRESH FOR EVEN MORE FLAVOUR

- Coriander leaves
- Basil leaves
- Rosemary
- Lemons and limes
- White onions

ACKNOWLEDGEMENTS

Firstly, to every single person that's purchased a copy of the Bored of Lunch books, and the incredible online community of millions. I can't put into words how much I appreciate you all.

Secondly, to anyone out there who's struggling to find that inner confidence to do something new or a make a change. I have zero professional kitchen experience or qualifications, and here I am writing my fourth cookbook. Back yourself and take the plunge, you never know what might happen.

Nathan x

1 3 5 7 9 10 8 6 4 2

Ebury Press,
an imprint of Ebury Publishing
20 Vauxhall Bridge Road
London SW1V 2SA

Ebury Press is part of the Penguin Random House
group of companies whose addresses can be found at
global.penguinrandomhouse.com

Text © Nathan Anthony 2024
Photography © Dan Jones 2024

First published by Ebury Press in 2024

www.penguin.co.uk

A CIP catalogue record for this book is available from the British
Library

ISBN 9781529914511

Commissioning Editor: Celia Palazzo
Production Director: Catherine Ngwong
Design: maru studio G.K.
Photographer: Dan Jones
Food stylist: Natalie Thomson
Prop stylist: Max Robinson

Printed and bound in Italy by LEGO SpA
The authorised representative in the EEA is Penguin Random House
Ireland, Morrison Chambers, 32 Nassau Street, Dublin D02 YH68.

'Life-changing recipes.'

Jess Clarke

'Quick, easy and even the kids want to help.'

Gemma Wheatland

'Has helped me lose 1½ stone, never used a cookbook so much.'

Scott Mc

'Amazing. Made my job as a parent easier.'

Maria Fowler

'Married 20 years and my husband only started cooking with these books.'

Kim Lock